THE SECOND TABLE

Where Compromise is Not an Option and Honesty
is a Non-Negotiable

HOPE MOQUIN

FOREWORD

The book that you are holding in your hands is a book for every single person on this Earth. It's a book that goes 'there.' It's a vulnerable and comforting "Me too." at a time where our world needs it most.

I met Hope, three years ago at Divine Women's Conference at Free Chapel in Gainesville, Georgia. I was a new mom of my then three-month old son, Luca. All while I was desperate to get out of my yoga pants and out of my house to be filled with the goodness of God. I had never attended Divine before, but there was a pulling on my soul that I couldn't deny and I knew I needed to be there. The weekend of the conference arrived and my husband was in Seattle for work which left me no other option than to bring Luca along. I can't lie, on the drive I almost turned around at each exit I passed convincing myself that I'd be better off spending the evening at home. When we arrived I got out of the car, strapped my baby carrier on and nervously walked inside. On this specific night, Bethel Music was leading worship. I am not sure about you but I feel the presence of God most strongly during worship and I was in full anticipation for what I would experience. One song in and the tears began to roll down my cheeks. It was everything that I needed. It was the perfect moment, until Luca began to cry. I tried to bounce him, feed him, shh-ssh him, all the Mom tricks. But nothing was working. I reached down to grab my diaper bag to leave when I felt a gentle hand on my shoulder.

I turned around to see the kindest face of a beautiful young woman and she said to me "Hi, you may think this is weird, but I've been watching you and it seems like you have your hands full. So I just wanted to offer to hold your baby for you so that you can really take this moment in. My name is Hope and I am a student here. I'm volunteering this weekend and I would love to lend you a helping hand." The new, overprotective mom in me wanted to say "Thank you so much for your offer, but I'm okay." However, I knew that I had two choices: 1) I either accepted this help (and asked her to stand where I could see her, lol) or 2) To head home listening to Bethel music in the car, with a screaming child, all while trying to convince myself that it was better than the real thing. If you're wondering what happened from there I'll keep it short: Hope held my son, I cried more tears with my arms lifted high, and we sat in the lobby and shared life stories until they kicked everybody out. And the rest is history.

I think this story is a good example of how God shows up in our everyday lives. In this specific scenario, He put the desire in my heart to attend Divine. He also knew that there were going to be barriers to this actually happening for me. A newborn son with no option other than to bring him along (at bedtime, may I add) and a husband who was out of town for work. I had to make the decisions as God always allows us to do. He isn't a forceful God that pushes his power on us. He allows us to make decisions for ourselves. Yet, He is always there ready to make our journey easier and less painful and to welcome us home with open arms. The decisions I had to make were, "Do I stay home or do I faithfully trust the desire in my heart and God's voice and go anyway?" As we now know from the story, God orchestrated all of the steps of that evening. He knew, before I did, that He was going to provide exactly what I needed as long as I made the decision to go and trust Him.

I don't know about you, but I see God show up a lot in this way. In the beginning of my relationship with Him, I still wanted to resist. I wanted to see how much I could do, handle and plan on my own. I will be the first to admit, that it gets tiring really fast. Still to this day, I have never had a better plan for myself or my family than God has for us. The peace that comes when we let Go and let God (as cliché and bumper sticker-y as that sounds) is a real thing, my friends. I find myself in conversation with God all day long as I am waking in the early hours of the day to care for our two beautiful children (God, please give me the strength and energy to make it through this day), as I make decisions as to where to spend my time (God, please give me the wisdom to make the most beneficial use of this time), and in the simple, quiet and calm moments (God, thank you for this moment and for these people that you have blessed my life with.) I think sometimes we can get intimidated that we have to show up in some kind of professional way to get God's attention when the truth is, God wants to meet us exactly where we are. Struggling, tired, worn out, confused and _____. That's one of the (many) things that makes God the loving, accepting Father that He is.

Friends, I am so excited for you to experience the love, compassion and wisdom that is inside of the pages of this book. I've had the honor of sitting at the table with Hope for the last few years. She is as pure and as real as they come. She loves and celebrates people the way that Jesus does. You don't have to keep forcing your seat at a table that isn't accepting of all that you are, all that you deserve, and all that God says you are. There's room for us all at The Second Table, and I can't wait to see you there.

Xo, Grace Allen

TABLE OF CONTENTS

ACKNOWLEDGMENTS

To Larry Moquin:

My dad. Thank you for always being my number one fan in everything I have put my foot towards. You have exemplified what a true man of God looks like and you have shown up for me in every way I haven't been able to show up for myself. You are my biggest fan and I will always be yours, too. Thank you for all your prayers you kept praying even when I didn't want them. I am who I am because of you.

To Pastor Blake and Laura Hamon:

Thank you for believing in me. In seasons where every seat in my life were empty, you both showed up to fill one every time. I learned grace because of you and your family. I learned consistency because of you and your family. I learned what family meant because of you and your family. I wouldn't have made it to where I am if it weren't for you two. I love your family like my own. Thank you for giving me a chance when nobody else would. Thank you for saying yes to Jesus, so I could say yes to Him, too.

To Free Chapel College:

All my students. Thank you for inspiring me to be my best. Being one of the directors here has been my greatest joy and upmost honor. I love each and every one of you to your core and there is not a thing I wouldn't stop and do for any of you. I see myself in so many of you and it pushes me to always extend grace that much more. If God can do it in me, He can do it in you. Run and chase your dreams. You'll get there, I promise.

ACKNOWLEDGMENTS

To Clark From the Streets in Atlanta:

Thank you for showing me purpose. Clark may never see this, but I met Clark one night when my friends and I stopped to talk with the homeless. Clark reignited something in my soul for the broken. Clark was homeless but knew the Word of God more than most people I know. There was something about this man that gave me the recognition of the Gospel being made for the streets, not just the walls.

PREFACE

We are not suppose to have it all together.

The only reason this truth is deep rooted within me is because at one time, I spent months - and I mean months, breaking myself in pieces trying to perfect every detail of my life. When I fell short, I panicked and grabbed whatever was in arms reach and I booked it. I'm not even a runner and I would sprint away. I hid for weeks mourning at what I had done. In disbelief I had fallen once again. Terrified to face the world again and was unsteady in the fact I had no idea what relationship with Jesus really meant.

You see, I sat down at this table once. Everyone was wearing masks and had their luggage next to them. However, it was zipped up so no one could see what was inside of this seemingly perfect looking baggage. They told me following Jesus meant to never do wrong. Because if you trip even a little, then that meant you never loved Him to begin with. And it wasn't long before I was shoved out from my seat. My life was too messy to try to put on a mask to fit in. My shortcomings were too heavy to try and carry them with me at the bottom of my bag. I wasn't comfortable in wearing a mask, because even if I tried, I knew what was really going on inside of me.

I walked alone for a bit, but I was not lonely. Just because you are alone at times, does not mean you are lonely. I was walking with Jesus trying to figure out what the heck it actually meant to be close to Him. Because I couldn't bring myself to believe perfection was it. While walking, I came across another table. Everyone was bare-faced and had their luggage next to them unzipped and wide opened. They were each taking turns reaching down into their baggage and pulling out their mistakes. And I watched each time as they tossed them behind their shoulder one by one.

This table. I sat down at this table, and I stayed. Without having to try to hide my shortcomings. Instead, we shared ours and even slapped our knees laughing about a few. Because some mistakes are so undoubtably insane that you have no choice but to laugh at them. This table didn't try to perfect themselves. They embraced our imperfectness. Then we moved forward to what was ahead. Not glued to our mess ups. You see, loving Jesus isn't contingent on whether or not we mess up. Loving Jesus is acknowledging we fell short, (even if it is yet again. Trust me, I know all about that) and choosing to get right back up. Christianity isn't perfection, my friend. We are not called to have it all together. We are going to mess up and we are going to fall.

Choose to get back up.

We can hide out and beat ourselves up for messing up, of course. But when it's all said and done, God is still God. He forgives. He doesn't disown what is His. So yeah, we can mourn in it for weeks, but we will come to the conclusion that it's time to move forward because there is such ahead. But the question that sat deep in my soul in one season was, how much time are we going to let go to waste in the duration? He already forgave us. It's up to us when we choose to get back up. It's up to us to pull up our mistake, look at it, maybe laugh about it, and toss it over our shoulder. There's so much ahead. Now go get it, friend.

And hey, just for the books – I am still sitting at the second table. Everyday.

"Now it happened, as Jesus sat at the table in the house, that behold, many tax collectors and sinners came and sat down with Him and His disciples. And when the Pharisees saw it, they said to His disciples, "Why does your Teacher eat with tax collectors and sinners?" When Jesus heard that, He said to them, "Those who are well have no need of a physician, but those who are sick. But go and learn what this means: 'I desire mercy and not sacrifice.' For I did not come to call the righteous, but sinners, to repentance."

Matthew 9:9-13 (NKJV)

INTRODUCTION

In the eighth grade, I discovered this gift of writing but never began to write until I was eighteen. A hard season drove me to the pen and paper and looking back, I wouldn't trade it for the world. Which is how a lot of ache turns out to be. Ache is gain. And I believe our ache is the greatest piece we have to offer to people. I haven't always done it right and I most certainly haven't always gotten it right. But I absolutely have failed my way forward and I have come to a place where my failure has been my most prized possession. Many books I've read and I have refrained from writing my own because I refused for it be as the other ones on the shelves. I think the words I'll share are risky, and maybe that's why I've put it off for so long. I believe in raw transparency and hard truth that is sometimes reality. I don't believe in sugar coating or beating around the bush. My heart is that whoever reads these words feel the human emotion in each story, in each failure, and in each recommitment.

My whole life I have heard, "You have so much potential" and even now, I catch myself telling particular people, "You have so much potential." The hard reality to those words is that even with the best intention those words are empty words. For a long time, I was tired of people telling me I had potential because I had no clue what that meant. I didn't know if that was a good thing or an underlying insult. Whatever this potential people talked about was, I didn't see it nor did I want to. But through all the mess, I came to know a God who showed me this potential people told me I had was not ever something I was going to put on one day. It was something I already had. That was given to me from the one who made me. All because he loved me. So here's a little about me that I hope can create some commonality between us.

I know what it's like to wait in expectation for something my intuition knows will never happen. I know what it's like to invest your whole being into someone desperate for them to do the same, but never happens. I know what it's like to love someone who you are unsure if they will even make it to see tomorrow because they're an addict. And I know what it's like to feel everything for someone only to have them feel the exact same but for someone else (dramatic eighteen year old me) (but those feelings still count, too). I know what it's like to be the cheater, and I know what it's like to be the one cheated on. I know what it's like to take months building your trust for someone just for them to unexpectedly rip it out from under your feet when you're not looking. I know what it's like to have everything in the palm of my hand and then to lose it within days. I know what it's like to find yourself in the backseat of a cop's car wondering how your life ended up in that direction. And I know what it's like to sit in and out of counseling. I know what it's like to be at the top and I know what it's like to the be at the darkest bottom, close to God and far from God.

I know what it's like to be human, and feel really human things. And I've learned that if there's one thing I don't want to do in life it's pretend that I've always had it all together. Because that was never the case. So here I am, welcoming you into my really messy life where in the piles of heartache and the loads of uncertainty, you can see an overwhelming depiction of God's grace and faithfulness surrounding each step. Walking through it was like a blurry hell, but now looking back, my eyes are widened and all I can say is, "Wow, who would have thought that such a big God could be so quietly clever."

So my friend, listen. All cards on the table for a minute. I don't know a lot of things, but one thing I am sure of is that we all can relate to one another. And if you refuse to believe so, you can rest on the fact that you are human. As am I, therefore we can stand on the commonality of that together. We don't come from the same home, and we don't have the same dreams. Our scars look very different, and our perspectives are probably on opposite ends of the map. We don't have the same story and where you are walking is by no means a spitting image of where I am walking. And that, well that is the beauty of it.

We're all different, but we're all human. We're all human, but we've all tripped a few times. And we've all tripped a few times, but we're all human. Together — in this comical gift that we call life. A passion for people has not always been here. In fact, in my younger days I hated the human race. I didn't believe people were worth investing my time into because of society's ulterior motive. I remained closed off and silent. But I have hope (no pun intended). I have hope in humanity. I believe we're all walking, sometimes sprinting, through our snippet of existence just trying to figure out what step is right. But I can tell you that even if the step you're taking isn't the most comfortable step, that I am so proud of you for putting your foot out and trying. I believe in elevating others. I believe in loving with no depraved motive. In getting back up and brushing off our scraped knees. I believe in bold dreams and I stand firm that there is hope for everybody, regardless of what it may look like from the surface level. My goal is for us to drop this "Whoever gets to the finish line first wins" nonsense. Let's be kind. Let's speak life. Let's love. Let's help build dreams, not overtake them.

You see, for a long time written words were all that I had. And now, I want to use them for others who may only have them as well.

I never attended a University or anything like that, but I remember sitting at this coffee bar at a local college waiting on my friend to get out of class. This was the first time I recognized my deep desire to know humanity. I was watching all of these students walk by and most of them looked so dry in the face. As if there was no purpose they were striving towards. Looking back, I don't know what on Earth I would have done if I ever went to a huge school because knowing myself now, I am a "get to know every single person that walks by" kind of girl. And I would have been terribly overwhelmed at a big school because I would never have gotten the chance to meet everyone. In the world we live in today it is so uncommon that people want to get to know other people and I always catch myself staring at someone while we make that awkward eye contact then I feel my palms behind to sweat and I want to crawl in a hole.

The poor kid probably thinks I'm hard core judging him when really I'm just trying to figure out what kind of person he is and what he's thinking and the potential he has (Again with the potential. What does that even mean?) Or sometimes, I'm honestly just thinking about if they know Jesus or not. And if not, well then they're about to hear about Him. Just kidding. Kind of. I mean, do you even know me? Of course I'm about to see if they know the Lord.

My mind is always thinking beyond the surface. You know, the innermost things, I want to know. I don't know why but that's just how I'm wired. Very observant. Observant but at the same time my mind is always racing a million miles per hour and I find it very difficult to stay on one certain topic, and I get off track very easily. That's why I love writing so much, because the pen in my hand reaches the paper and sometimes it just doesn't stop. And that's okay with me, because words inspire me. There's just something about them that are so comforting. Can they hurt? Most definitely. They can cause the most detrimental strike in our minds yet multitudinously secure the sincerities of our hearts. For me, words were what held me together in the darkest of times. When I felt as if the world was toppled on top of me and every human being's motive was to harm me, I had words.

Words that I always desired to speak but could never build the courage to do so. Words that could hopefully express what all I was feeling when more than most was literally quite nothing. Words that could just maybe save me if someone had heard them. Words that I held dear to my heart. I had thousands of words sitting at the tip of my tongue but somehow could never make their way to depart from my lips. Verbally communicating what I felt? Deathly. I couldn't bare the thought. I could yell and I could defend myself and others. I could rant on about irrelevant subjects. I could talk and talk all day long but when it came to feelings.. I would have rather die. Standing face to face with humanity in vulnerability terrified me.

And so I wrote.

Never did I really discover how sacred writing was to me until life knocked me to the bottom of the valley in one season. It's funny to me how the outcome of heartbreak and how the outcome of pain can result in finding yourself a little bit more. I went through a painful heart break that I knew was going to end in despair from day one (I've found that a lot of us have gone through this. Which means we will get along great because most of my poor decisions started like this). Yes, I am one of those people who sadly enough have to learn the hard way. And trust me, I have had my fair share of learning the hard way with no one to blame but myself. But indeed, it is what it is and life does goes on.

During this dull season of my life, I had put myself in a place where I didn't have anyone to turn to. I was in a place where talking to God was what I wanted to sprint to but at the same time talking to God was something I wanted to dig a hole in and hide from. I was torn in between and everywhere I looked was fearful and left me feeling like a coward.

And so I wrote.

CHAPTER 1
THE ROOT: THE BEGINNING WE DON'T TALK ABOUT

My mother has always enjoyed writing, and I believe that is where I took it from. We share some of the same interests, however, disagreed on many things as well growing up. But I mean, are you even human if you never argued with your mom? At ten years old, twenty years old, and shoot, even thirty years old. We know how moms are. She always told me to watch out for the "bad friends" and the "bad guys" but from what I experienced, the church kids were the one's who seemed to be getting into trouble more so then the one's who weren't in church. And that, well, that was me.

"No, you can't stay the night with her because it's Saturday and we have church in the morning. End of discussion." was the blood boiling, god-awful response I received from my mom anytime I would ever try to hang out with my friends on the weekend when I was a child. Church was a non-negotiable. Whether I was getting dragged, paid (we'll get to that one later), bribed, any of those I was going. We were the family that was in church pews each Sunday and I was the kid who was at every Vacation Bible School and every youth group. I didn't despise it at the time. I mean, I grew up in it and remember attending for as long as I can remember. It was normal to me and I had not a clue of what life was like to not know of this man named Jesus. Was I saved? That's debatable. I acknowledged God and I was into this church world, but it was all a surface level type deal. Nothing intimate and nothing that widened my eyes and got me passionate. And I think to really say that you are saved and in love with Jesus is to be wide eyed and in awe of Him. To follow Him out of love and out of choice, not obligation out of all you know. But to really be in love, and commitment to Him. Not only to love Him, but to love others.

Which can be so hard, trust me, I know. The thing that really punched me in the face one day was the thought of this. God loves. That's literally it. The person who makes you want to scream at the top of your lungs and pull your hair out, He loves them. Just as much as He loves you. Not more than you, and not less than you. But equally. This overlooked truth had me re-evaluating my whole life and in utter shock for a while until I went to the Lord and asked Him to change my heart. This thought, or I should say this truth, it makes you think doesn't it?

People can be hard to love. I get it.

My mom and I were two polar opposites. She said white, I said black. She said up, I said down. She said yes, I said absolutely not. We had argued most of my life and we had many differences. A few years back, she was vacationing in West Palm Beach and sent me a good seventy five pictures of expensive stores and huge mansions. We were two polar opposites. She wanted a multimillion dollar mansion on the beach, and I wanted a small little townhouse in the suburbs. We're different and I would get so irritated with how she was. But it hit me one day. Real hard. Everybody is different. Your mom, your dad, your sibling, your best friend, your waitress, that stranger in front of you in line, the grocery clerk, everybody. Everybody is different. Which is how it's suppose to be. Yet, we have this tainted view of what we want people to look like and it is so wrong that we let our insides cringe at the innocence of who somebody is. Do we have to be buddy-buddy with everyone? No, and praise God for that.

But we do indeed need to love everyone.

Instead of looking at people with the lens of who we think they ought to be, how distinctively different would our conversations and our countenance be if we accepted that the person we are looking straight at is not the same as who we are, but rather they are their own person who is just as human as we are? It's life. No one is the same, but everybody is a person. A person who is undeserving of love, but who Christ calls to love anyways. And that is what love is.

WE'RE ALL HUMAN

Before I ever had this perspective I'll tell you that I grew up as a spoiled brat. Anything I wanted, I had. Anything I didn't care for, I didn't have. In good ole Acworth, Georgia I was always dressed as if I was walking the runway and in my own little mind I was certain that I ruled the world. I was living inside of my own skin as the person my parents had wanted me to be. Can you relate? I was that girl in elementary school who didn't ride the bus and who always had the newest name brand shirt. I was that girl who had the house that all my friends came over to every weekend, well, on the weekends that I wasn't at ballet rehearsal. Because I was that girl, too.

Middle school came around and I was actually the queen of back talking teachers. My parents were involved in my life, but at the same time they kind of weren't. They were very consumed in my brothers well being. Both of my parents had separate marriages before they came together and had me. My mom had a son with her first husband, and my dad had two sons and a daughter with his first wife. Technically, I'm an only child but the son from my moms first marriage grew up with me so I count him as the real-deal. My middle school years were an emotional rollercoaster in our family. Often, my parents would go on vacation and leave my brother and I home alone. We lived in a huge house so we would have people over to stay with us the whole time our parents were away. My brother would leave for days on end so my middle school friends and I would be in this huge house by ourselves most of the time. How we managed to never burn the house down? That remains unknown.

I never knew where my brother was at and never really asked. So much happened during this time that I am unsure of, but what I do know is that my brother ended up running away from home twice. The second time was a true tragedy. It was really the starting point in my own life spiraling downhill. On my thirteenth birthday I'll never forget the terror in my mothers eyes by the end of the night when we walked through the doors that evening. We were out in Atlanta all day celebrating my birthday and my brother refused to come with us that day. He ignored our calls all day but it wasn't anything unusual so we didn't put much thought into it.

Later in the evening I'll never forget walking in the house and up to my room. While putting my things away, the house stood still as I heard my mothers shriek fill every empty space. Her shriek was horrific and cold. I didn't know what was happening at the time and my dad brought me to my neighbors house across the street to stay there for the night. Confusion was wrapping itself around my mind. My eyes peaked out from the blinds on the window at my neighbors house as cop cars pulled in and out of my driveway. Come to find out, he had left a suicide note taped to my mothers mirror in her bathroom. And that was all that we had left from him.

Hours later of relentlessly searching for him throughout the night and next day, he was found in an abandoned house. He was alive but he was not sober. He was not a bad person, he was just a lost person. I do not believe there are such things as bad people. I do believe there are hurt people. Hurt people who are in drowning in desperation for an honest heart who has been hurt, too. However, it's one thing to let it be known you are hurting. It's one thing to let it be known that you are sad. It's one thing to let it be known that you are struggling. But through my experiences, I have seen firsthand in my own life and the lives of those close to me that vague practicality has never been a friend to a hurting heart.

I'm for the people who know what it's like to listen to their human heart over the still small voice and have it collapse in front of their face. I'm for the people who know what it's like to have everything in the palm of their hand and then to lose it within days. I'm for the people who have utterly to their core doubted their purpose. I'm for the people who have gotten so caught up in life they have neglected what they love. I'm for the people who have befriended the hole they dug themselves in. I'm for the people who almost took the easy way out of life. I'm for the people who know what it's like to be human, and feel really human things. Why? Because just like my brother in that season, I too, have known those things.

If we ever want to be effective people living effective lives then we cannot play it safe. We need raw, deep-rooted truth. I don't want people to feel as if they need to polish up their dirt before they talk about it. If you want to bring me your dirt, I want to sit down with you and hand you a flower pot.

Because listen, my friend. Good things that blossom, first, need dirt.
Raw as it is dirt.

I have learned to never go a day without carrying around a flower pot, and I am seeing firsthand what is inside is beginning to blossom naturally. Without having to clean it up. And so even if it's with shaky hands and wobbly steps, let's be people who aren't afraid to carry around a flower pot. Let's be people who are willing to carry someone else's, too. Because we never know who may need it.

GAINESVILLE, GEORGIA

After finding my brother, he was taken into one of those institutions for a few days. All of my parents attention focused on him, rightfully so. However, it left me hanging behind with no one but myself. And I still didn't really comprehend the severity of what was going on. All I knew was something was evidently different about him, and fear crept in when I was near him. He wasn't my brother that I knew him to be.

The next step was putting him into a Christian rehabilitation program in Tallahassee, Florida. Now, that was hard. If we all examine our lives, I believe we can pinpoint the time in our lives for which was the starting point of us going downhill. And this was mine. Sometimes, the only thing we have left inside of our bones is exactly that. Just us and our own human soul. And the only thing we have to offer is to just to show up. Empty-handed, confused, exhausted, fill in the blank.

It may feel as if complication is the the captain of your ship.
But show up, anyways.
It may feel as if your purpose has let the passenger seat call itself home.
But show up, anyways.
It may feel as if you're sailing on waves of uncertainty.
But show up, anyways.
It may feel as if the rain of burdens is drowning out your clarity.
But show up, anyways.

Because even amidst a storm the ship still sails. And we can either hide out in the back room or we can show up bold right smack in the middle of it. And if you stay, the storm has to run out of rain eventually. And when it starts to settle, you'll see that other side. It may be a little cloudy but what you're waiting for is there. It may be a little bit blurry, but it's still there. It may not be what you're expecting, but it's still there. And you are ruggedly on your way to meet it. Rugged or smooth. Show up, anyways. And that's what I admired about my brother in that season. Whatever the case was, he was showing up.

——————

Our family could only go and visit him once a month for a few hours. It didn't take a genius to notice how this effected my parents, but from all the mess that happened daily in our household, this program was what was best for all of us.

Eighth grade year started shortly before we got him into the program. I was in my last year of middle school and everything was going well for where I stood in my life. I was nervous that my brother wasn't at home anymore, because though we fought as every brother and sister do, he was my best friend and always had my back. He had been distant for a while leading up to his disappearance but before then, we were the best of friends. For instance, in sixth grade when I was the queen of starting drama I had a movie theater and buttered popcorn experience. There was this girl named Logan, she did not have the body figure of a sixth grader and the halls silenced with intimidation when she walked down them. If there was anybody in the school you did not want to piss off, it was her. Coincidentally, guess who pissed her off? Yep. This girl. Right here. Probably because I'm an enneagram 8.

In this particular situation my words had gotten twisted around and it got out that I was saying hateful things about her. It was all things I had thought at the time, but I dared not to ever speak them off my lips. Yet somehow, it got around I had everything in the world to say and I remember the day I almost had my face destroyed perfectly. I was in homeroom, in the back row and everyone was whispering to each other and glancing back at me. I speak with my facial expressions more than half the time and finally someone came up to me and told me Logan was coming after me when homeroom got out. Casually, I played it off like I could care less but inside I fell on the ground crying like a baby because I was petrified.

You guys don't know this girl and what she looked like and you don't know what I looked like either. I was absolutely terrified. All through homeroom you could see the fear on all of the faces as they all were telling me to be careful and how it'll go by quick. I just sat there sweating profusely trying to keep my cool. The bell rang and my eyes began to swell while my hands were quite literally dripping with sweat at this point. I stayed back so I could be the last one to leave. Everyone was out of the classroom and I ever so slightly peaked my head out the door. Just like the movies, the whole entire sixth grade class was huddled around the end of the hallway and she was standing right smack in the middle waiting for me. Arms crossed, cleavage out of her undersized white t-shirt, hoop earrings, and teased hair.

While bullets of sweat shot out from my forehead in my bedazzled t-shirt and hair in braids, I gulped, and said not today Satan then quickly turned around back into class. My teacher walked with me all the way down the hall as I watched another teacher hold Logan back because she was about to come for me anyways. I was on my own when I got to the end of the hallway and as I was walking to gym with tears down my face everyone was coming up to me saying how teachers can't stop her after school.

I started hyperventilating because I was a twig in middle school, I talked so much but I would get snapped in half if anyone ever laid a hand on me back then. I called my brother in the locker room and he said he would be there in ten minutes. So I got my stuff, told everyone I had a dentist appointment and waited in the front office for him. For the record, I'm pretty sure he got there a lot sooner than ten minutes. My brother always had my back, and I could count on him. Not having him in eighth grade year after everything that had panned out was different. To top it off not even a month in, my parents had told me we were moving to Gainesville, Georgia. What the heck. We hardly had much of a relationship in this time of my life so to be told we were making a move as drastic as that was absurd to me.

We had been driving two hours up there every Sunday for a church we were attending, but I never imagined we would move there. Mom and Dad were committed to this church and talked about all the time. Right smack in the middle of Gainesville. Apparently it was a well known church and the Pastor was one of the best they've ever heard. I didn't know much about it, and at my age I didn't really care. I didn't want to move again. We always moved houses but always close in the area, never too far away.

A few weeks passed and as much as I didn't like it (as if my thirteen year old self was really going to be the final say in moving), we were settled in our new house. I was at my new school and quickly meeting new people there and at church. These kids were very different from my friends back home, and I can't say that was a good thing. Moving to Gainesville changed me. I left everything I knew, and picked up everything new. My brother was still in the program and my parents were busy with him, the new house and work. So I was just me. I had the whole downstairs to myself, I was meeting new people, and I was taking a risk with new territory. And none of those three were of my benefit.

IDENTIFYING AND UPROOTING

This season was the root of many behaviors I would befriend and the reasoning behind why I was the way that I was. We all have a root or even multiple roots. The crazy part is so many us get frustrated with ourselves in how we react and how we behave, but then we don't time to backtrack and ask the Lord to show us where it all began. So many of us don't understand why we do some of the things we don't want to do. Why certain responses set something off inside our souls. Why some words that seem so small hurt so deeply. Why we run towards things that we know aren't good for us. You know who understood this? Paul.

"For I do not understand my own actions. For I do not do what I want, but I do the very thing I hate. Now if I do what I do not want, I agree with the law, that it is good. So now it is no longer I who do it, but sin that dwells within me. For I know that nothing good dwells in me, that is, in my flesh. For I have the desire to do what is right, but not the ability to carry it out. For I do not do the good I want, but the evil I do not want is what I keep on doing. Now if I do what I do not want, it is no longer I who do it, but sin that dwells within me."
Romans 7:15-20 (ESV)

Yes! These words are actually in the Bible. There are humans who struggled with the same things you and I struggle with. Paul writes, "For I have the desire to do what is right, but not the ability to carry it out." Talk about relatable. There are many habits you and I carry in which we don't necessarily like. There are ways you and I react in which we know are not holy. There are mindsets you and I have in which we know are not beneficial for us. There are things instilled in our human nature in which we do not have the ability to carry out what is right. Which is one of the reasons why there is such a need for God and his grace in humanity. There is a God who is bold and who is big. A God who is sitting on the edge of his seat waiting for us to open our hands and simply say, "I need you, God." That is his joy. Helping our frail human hearts and eyes see our roots. All for the purpose of allowing our human heart to know him a little bit more.

For me, if I can be very honest, let me tell you about when I was younger and had Field Trips. Any Field Trip that came up, I still remember that seven year old girl with bouncy brown curls going up to my mom and batting those eyes asking if she would come with me. And every time, I remember there being something else. In my little mind, I took her not ever coming with me as her not wanting to spend time with me with the things I enjoyed. And that led me to wonder if the things I enjoyed were not good enough for people. This is not a bash on my mother by any means. Every individual has areas in their lives where they were hurt by their parents. Why? Because we are all human. You and I ought to give more grace to our parents. They are human, too. Just like you and I, they didn't always get it right.

I realized when I was twenty year old, that my whole life I grew up hiding the things I was interested in from people because I didn't want people to not want to hang out with me. I would get my favorite book and literally drive to places that were secluded so I wouldn't see anyone I knew while I was reading. Because in my mind, I allowed the enemy to feed it with thoughts like *"What kind of loser likes reading?"* Those thoughts were my reality. If we aren't careful, we can master the art doing things we love by ourselves and build a wall so high that it would be impossible for someone to join even if they wanted to.

In the season where we had to put my brother into the Program, my home was a broken home. My parents attention was fully on him, which looking back it needed to be, but in my twelve year old mind all I could comprehend was irrelevancy and rejection. I felt pushed to the side, so the first boy I met who showed deep interest in me, I grabbed onto it for dear life (I'll get to that later). Because we are human and we all crave acceptance.

What's your root? Maybe it's the way your mom or dad wasn't there for you the way you wanted them to be. Maybe it's a sibling who treated you like dirt, or who was always in the spotlight while you were left in the dust. Maybe it's from kids in elementary school not included you in recess. Maybe it's from a family member, or friend. Maybe it's from a Pastor. Ouch. That's a really real one, too. The thing about roots is they are often formed from experiences that were out of our control. There was not anyway to prevent the way that someone rejected us, and there was not anything we could do about the actions of others. We cannot prevent the actions of others but we can control our responses. Though the way the root was created is out of our control, the way we go back and shed light on the root is our choice.

I don't know what your root may be, but ask the Lord to show you. One thing that I have learned is that the Lord will not ever reveal something that He does not intend to heal. What is was, does not always have to be. Be bold. Ask God with an expectancy to show you. No more cycles. No more acting out of character. Let's tell these walls, "Sorry, but you can't stay up anymore."

And just for the kicks, let's smirk a little bit while they tremble down.

HONEST TRUTH

"Are you tired? Worn out? Burned out on religion? Come to me. Get away with me and you'll recover your life. I'll show you how to take a real rest. Walk with me and work with me—watch how I do it. Learn the unforced rhythms of grace. I won't lay anything heavy or ill-fitting on you. Keep company with me and you'll learn to live freely and lightly."

Matthew 11:28-30 (MSG)

CHALLENGE

I feel like life can get so loud and in our face at times that all we need is someone there to hear us. I don't want us to live a life that was worth nothing. A life that knew the world but didn't know the people. I want to know the people with intentionality. Authenticity, too. With opening our heart to others, and hearing theirs. With sharing our shortcomings in hope that whoever is listening won't fall the same as we did. In celebrating valleys and the people we meet through them. We don't have to strive to be everything to everybody, but let's just be something to somebody. Reach out to someone in your life, or even a stranger you may meet this week, and let them know how proud of them you are. Go out of your way to create a conversation that is welcoming for authenticity and watch how the conversation flourishes.

REFLECTION

I. How would you describe your current relationship with God? More on the surface level side or the widened eyes and passionate side?

II. Is there someone in your life who you have been looking at with the lens of who you think they ought to be rather than accepting them as their own person who is just as human as you are? Why do you think you feel the way you do?

III. What is your family dynamic like? How has it played a role in who you are today?

IV. If you could pinpoint the time in your life that you believe was the starting point of your ache, what would that be? How has that effected the way you live your life today?

V. Are there any behaviors you are carrying that you would like to identify the root of? How have these behaviors effected you and the people around you?

CHAPTER 2

ANGRY OVER THE OUTCOME VS. ANGRY ABOUT OUR SIN

"Is he following us?"

"Don't stop. Just keep driving."

"Uh, I think we should stop."

"Keep driving."

Sirens go off, lights go on

"I'm so sorry, Hope"

At fourteen I fell head over heels for this boy. Now that, that was one hell of a piece of my life. By hell, I really mean actual hell. However, my fourteen year old heart was emotionally convinced into believing that it was love and lost myself in the midst of it. Our relationship was unhealthy in every way, shape, and form. There was not a single person who support-ed us together, but we were inseparable and no matter how much chaos we caused we still managed our way back to each other despite the pain it caused everyone around us. Everyone who has been in an unhealthy rela-tionship clap your hands! *Handclaps* Almost three years we spent to-gether and no, it did not end happily ever after. But I do believe with all my heart that it shaped a big portion of who I am today, and for that I am only thankful. We choose how we use our ache. Even as deep as an ache it may be.

Rewind a little bit. Sunday morning came around, and we all know what meant. Church. I remember riding in the car having a million different thoughts flood my mind. I had never talked to this boy in person that I was meeting that day, we had only texted a few times so I was embarrassingly nervous. (Typical millennial, right?) It all happened so fast and we barely knew anything about each other, but there was something about him that I was so drawn to. Looking back, I see that root where my parents had unin-tentionally pushed me to the side and he was someone who didn't. He pursued me and was adamant towards me to have me. And take note, I met this boy at church.

CHURCH DOESN'T MAKE PEOPLE GOOD

Just because someone goes to church does not mean squat. So many times I hear people say, "Oh yeah, they go to church so they're good." Or, "I met them on this app that is actually used for hook ups, but their bio says Philippians 4:13 so they obviously love the Lord."

First of all, I may step on some toes with this but I really don't care because it's necessary to hear. Anyone who has a deep understanding of who they are in Christ will not have any desire to meet someone on an app that was originally used for hook ups. Don't be fooled. Wait and get to know someone's character outside the four walls. Wait to get to know someone's heart outside of an app that has destructive intentions.

That Sunday I met the boy was the day that started, and quite frankly was the day that changed everything. Do I share all these tiny details because my heart is still attached to him? Not by any means. I share these details because I want you to feel where I'm coming from and for it to not just be empty words. Listen to me, at whatever your age may be. If none of your family or friends are supportive of your significant other, take notice to that. Don't sweep it under the carpet. As wild as it may sound, they see what you can't see. Please don't make the mistake as I did and mute your mind to the feedback of your loved ones. We need our loved ones more than we think.

If they don't support our significant other based off biased opinions and lack of effort to get to know them, then that is a different story.

But if they don't support our significant other based off actual facts and huge red flags, let's notice that. We need another set of eyes that aren't blurred with infatuation. I promise you. It's a beautiful thing to find someone who makes your world seems as if it's on pause, someone who makes you feel as if nothing wrong will ever happen again. It's a beautiful thing for two people to come together and build a relationship, to open up and discover things about yourself that they bring out of you. But it's not a beautiful thing when we're blindsided by characteristics we couldn't see when we first met him/her. And it's not a beautiful thing having to deal with heartache even years after the relationship ends.

This was my first relationship, prior to this I had not even held hands with a boy. I was as innocent as can be. I was naive. I believed that everything was pure, that everything was genuine. Not all teenage boys are as innocent. He was two years older than me and had experience in many ways I did not. Am I saying that it's wrong for two people to come together when their pasts don't line up? Not at all. I'm the BIGGEST advocate of messy pasts. Hence why I am writing this today. That's the beautiful part of love! Accepting one another despite the past. Although that comes with maturity, and a solid foundation in Christ. Which neither one of us had, therefor it was evident to which direction our relationship was headed. Rock bottom (ha, ha).

FOURTEEN IN A COPS CAR

My parents were heavily involved in the church and with my brother, so I was really riding through life at this point by myself. This boy made me feel at home around him in a way I hadn't even felt in my own home. And that's exactly how the enemy creeps in. When we don't have a secure foundation in Christ the enemy will examine our lives and determine our most empty areas, and use things that seem good to fill those areas.

The enemy doesn't show up dressed up with horns and evidently evil. No, he shows up in things that seem to be an easy escape. In things that actually seem good from the surface level. Which is why the eyes of other people who have our best interest in mind are so important. Because when we are hurting we can't always see clearly. This boy dressed up manipulation in a way that seemed sweet. For a fourteen year old girl who had a complicated home life, when a boy who showed extreme interest made her seem like she was of value, she was easily bought in. Who wouldn't be?

On this particular night I knew that I was going to sneak out of my house and I was actually quite terrified. Isn't it funny how we know what we're getting ourselves into almost all of the time but then it comes as a shock when trouble occurs. When inwardly, we knew something poor was going to produce but our nagging flesh keeps pushing us ahead anyways. Then we end up in this hole with no one to pull us out, and we wonder why. In the brisk air of the middle of the night I found myself in a car with him and his two brothers. The brothers were both drinking while he was driving. We were all underage except for one of the brothers who bought the alcohol. None of us had our licenses and were driving this car. (Smart decisions with Hope part one). We went to this park down the road from my neighborhood and I remember feeling so shaky.

I didn't know why I was doing what I was doing. In my mind, I wasn't doing anything bad because I just wanted to spend time with this person who made me feel noticed, because I never experienced that before. I was always second choice, or not a choice at all in school. And he made it seem like I was first priority. His brothers were intoxicated through the roof so him and I were in the front seats. We were about a mile away from my neighborhood and I was about to get away with it when we saw the lights start flashing behind us. And in about two minutes my entire life changed. While hiding their alcohol the brothers were telling him to keep driving. I didn't know what to do. Tears flooded my eyes because I knew I just got caught. They were not sad tears, they were angry tears. Because *I was mad about my outcome rather than being mad about my rebellion.* I was a ballerina with straight A's who had never faced trouble before. And then it came time when were driving away from the officer for too long and had no choice but to pull over. Just in my favor, we pulled into my neighborhood and I will never forget the sound of these empty words that so many of us would come to hear again in our lives over and over, "I'm so sorry."

And my heart sat still.

The officer looked inside and his eyes widened while he demanded we all step out of the vehicle. He kept asking if I was okay as if I was taken without consent. Granted, it was two in the morning and I was a fourteen year old girl in a car with three boys who looked much older than me. He escorted me over to his car and made sit in the back behind bars and instructed that I call a parent to come get me. I remember sitting there looking down at my phone and then looking back up through the bars on the window. Fourteen in a cop's car I wiped my tears off my screen as I picked it up to call my parents. And I knew that this moment would change the direction of my life. Which, indeed I was actually right about.

Within minutes, I saw my dad swing his car around next to us. To this day, I had never seen him so angry. I saw fire in his eyes as he tripped over his feet trying to get out of the car and went straight for the oldest brother. I swear to this day I thought he was going to kill him. Then I saw the officer jump over to hold him back. He was so angry. The officer calmed him down and directed him over to me, and my heart sunk. The door opened and the officer told me I'm free to go home. When in reality, I wanted nothing more but to stay. My feet slowly got out of the car and walked to my dad's car. We drove away in silence. Walking into my home I was greeted by shouts from my mother, "What were you thinking?!" Oh, I thought it was never going to end. I sat on the couch across from them both and I wept. The ugly weep, where snot was coming out like Niagara Falls. Thousands of thoughts and hundreds of emotions I couldn't form into words.

And so I wrote.

THE NECESSITY OF BOUNDARIES

I had never heard them yell the way they did that night and all I felt was numb. I knew they were going through hell with my brother and now their other child was seemingly a mess. And if we want to backtrack, we'll see this all started because I didn't have any boundaries set in my life. Nor was I ever taught what a boundary meant. But to dig a little deeper. How would I even know what boundary to set if I didn't even know the root to what my problem was? It's a weighty process, friend. But it's a process well worth it. First, we determine our root. Second, based off our roots we examine what areas of our lives now need boundaries to keep that root uprooted. Without boundaries, we are leaving our soil open for that same seed to be planted that we spent so much time digging up.

What even is a boundary?

Well, boundaries. My first thought when I heard of this word was I don't know what those are but they don't sound fun. The actual definition of a boundary is a line that marks the limits of an area. Also known as a dividing line. Throughout our lives, as briefly mentioned earlier, I'm sure we can all point out habits we kept falling back into and could never figure out why we kept getting involved with things that hurt us. Things that would hinder us. Things that would keep us from where God was trying to take us. Now, I'm an enneagram 8. So especially after pointing out and realizing these things, I had to figure out what the heck my problem was. (and all my 8's said... AMEN).

I wanted to know why I was the way I was, why I reacted to things the way I reacted, why I responded to hurt the way I did, why specific things triggered specific emotions — I wanted to know all of it. *Because when you care about where you're going, you care about the habits that could keep you getting there.* And what I learned was that boundaries are a heck of a lot more important than we think. Boundaries in relationships, in places, in people, in habits, in thoughts. They matter. They shape you. They keep you true to you.

So, let's talk really real for a minute.

Everyone has different boundaries they set up or different doors they have shut in their life. Whether that be in a past relationship, drinking, sexual temptation, family members, friendships, or any sort of habits. We all have struggles and we all have tried at some extent to help them. Here's the thing, if a boundary was created in the first place then there is a reason as to why we created it. We don't create something that is meant to help us and just go for a few weeks then remove it. Unless if the Lord has deliberately told us that it's good for us to take it off — we keep that boundary in place. Because it was created to help us.

Let me ask you. How do you not cross the line that you drew? Well, you don't even look at the line. You keep your mind set on things above. You keep your eyes on where you're headed. You don't flirt with the line that was drawn. If we used to struggle with alcohol and we don't want to drink, then why do we think we can handle going to that party? If we don't want to go too far sexually, then why do we think we can handle being alone in a room together at late hours? Oh yes, let's get to the nitty gritty. If we don't want to get sucked back into a bad relationship, then why do we think we can start casually hanging out again? No, friend. If you don't want to cross that line then care about yourself to not even look at the line.

If we set a boundary in our life it's because there was a necessary need for one.

We don't set a boundary just to go back in a few months and remove it because all of a sudden "We can handle it." The biggest lie in my life has been, "I can handle it." Because I know God, and I know my morals. So I can go and do these things and I can handle it. Right? No! Wrong. How foolish of us. So deceiving and not true at all. More often than most, we put a stop to something because we feel like we're suppose to. As Christians, many of us put a boundary because we feel the Lord was leading us to so he could take us higher. How beautiful is it that the God of the universe cares about us so much that he would take the time to intervene and prompt us to do something or more importantly, to *not* to something. Think about it. The God who breathed life into every lung, the God who is the creator of all things, the God who we know as Lord and as friend — if He takes the time to get our attention about something, it MUST be because He has a purpose in it.

People don't fall back into their old ways because they are bad people. A lot of people fall back into their old ways because they knocked a door that the Lord specifically shut. They kept pushing and pushing and eventually their own human hands opened back up the door that was shut to protect them. I've said it before, but I don't personally believe there are "bad" people. Sure, we were all born into a sinful world therefore we are inherently human. But, I'm talking about the people who are lost. The people who are caught up in cycles and mistakes. They aren't bad people. They are people who don't have a clear vision for their life. When you have a vision, you don't want to keep running back. Yeah it hurts sometimes, but you want to keep running forward.

I know, here I am sounding whack again. I feel like I have such a different view than what is cheered for. But stick with me.

No one wakes up and decides, "Hey, I'm going to be a drug addict one day."
No one wakes up and decides, "Hey, I really want to get sucked back into my toxic relationship."
No one wakes up and decides, "Hey, I think I'm going to go too far sexually with that person today."
No one wakes up and decides, "Hey, I'm going to have one drink tonight and I'll be fine even though I use to struggle with it."
No one wakes up and decides, "Hey, I'm going to let this person back in my life and it's going to be fine."

You better believe that I did not wake up and decide that I wanted to end up in the backseat of a cop car at fourteen.

People don't dream about being caught up in something that is killing their soul. But people end up in things like that because they didn't know where they were going to begin with. OR people end up in things like that because they knew *exactly* where they were going and they didn't set up the necessary boundaries to keep them on the right track to get there. When we know our vision of where we are going, it makes it a lot easier to make decisions. When we care about what God is doing more than what our flesh wants to be doing, it makes sense to say no to settling. When we care about who God is shaping us to be, it's easier to shut down anything that may hinder that.

When we begin to care about what God is doing — we begin to care about what we are doing.

I don't know about you but I don't want to run full speed ahead of God and tell Him to catch up with me. I want to sit back with Him and let Him show me what lines I need to draw to keep me in place. And I don't want to step over those lines unless He takes my hands and walks with me over them. I wish someone would have told me this at a young age. My fourteen year old heart NEEDED to be educated on healthy boundaries. In this time, I thought I was completed by this boy and I knew my parents were going to separate us. Which meant I was being stripped of the only thing I knew to identify with. And I was right. Looking back, I can't blame them. What would you do if your fourteen year old daughter pulled a stunt like that? You just try to do the right thing.

But sometimes even the right thing doesn't heal. For me, it broke me. But praise God it broke me. Praise God we have experienced things that have completely shattered our souls. Praise God everything we were has been entirely broken in half before. Why would you say that, Hope?

Because. When everything we are is shattered we then have all the room in the world for the Lord to build us back up in everything who He is. There's no room for shaky foundations anymore because we are built on the rock.

On this night I remember shamefully walking downstairs and laying in my bed for days. I hated what I did, but I hated the fact that they separated us more than what I had done. And friend, let me tell you that it is a dangerous place for us to be in when we become angry over the outcome from our own decisions more than we become angry from our sin that got us there in the first place. God cannot operate and move in our hearts when we are angry we got caught rather than broken that we messed up.

Peter and Judas both denied Jesus. Judas wept because he got caught. Peter wept because he messed up. Judas wept because he regretted his actions. Peter wept because he wanted to repent. Two men, two similar situations, two different outcomes. I don't know about you, but I want to be found like Peter.

The Second Table

HONEST TRUTH

"Jesus heard about it and spoke up, "Who needs a doctor: the healthy or the sick? I'm here inviting outsiders, not insiders—an invitation to a changed life, changed inside and out."

Luke 5:31-32 (MSG)

CHALLENGE

Watching as integrity was tossed across the room and as loneliness was either stepped on or stepped over. Almost as if being lonely was just how it was suppose to be. I stared into the depths of what it looked like to live in this distinctive way with no vision. I didn't believe that there was such a thing as greater purpose. But what I had learned is that the heart of God was not for us to curl up next to society's best friend named ordinary. But rather, to take what he had made and to use it.

Everything begins to make sense when we take a minute to pause, and open the door to what the Lord has in His house. To stop tirelessly fighting for a space in normality where we will inwardly feel so, so out of place. Self evaluate your life in this moment to determine if there are any areas where you are quietly fighting for a place in normality. Take a step back and ask yourself, "Is this really what I want?" Or more importantly, "Is this really what I need?"

REFLECTION

I.   Has there ever been a relationship or friendship in your life that your family and friends tried to warn you about? If yes, how did you respond to their concern? What did you learn from it?

II. Have you ever participated in something that you knew you shouldn't have? What were the repercussions? How could you have avoided that outcome?

III. What does a boundary mean to you? What boundaries don't you have set that you need to have set?

IV. Has there been a person or habit in your life that you believed was making you feel complete, but now looking back, you see that you never were actually complete like you thought? How has that effected you today? How can you learn from this?

CHAPTER 3

WHY CHURCH WASN'T FOR ME

I did not meet Jesus from a sit down meeting of someone trying to put me in my place. I did not meet Jesus from someone trying to fix me and my problems. I did not meet Jesus from someone laying out in front of my face what is right and what is wrong. I did not meet Jesus from strict guidelines and rules. I did not meet Jesus from a Christian being hateful towards me with good intentions.

To spice this story up a little bit, my parents made me have a meeting and talk to my Youth Pastors, Blake and Laura, about what had happened. Talk about embarrassment. I wasn't unaware of God. I was actually close to falling into full commitment with God before I met this boy. I actually wrote my first sermon at twelve years old. I wrote how I never did drugs, and how I never drank, and how I never slept around. I wrote about how one day I was going to speak and I was going to be able to share how I stood firm and pure through the years. Isn't that wild? However, my story now looks very different than the words I wrote at thirteen. But I'm very okay with that. Because it's God's story.

You choose how you let life effect you. Blake and Laura knew I was involved in the church and so when I had to sit down and share about what I had done it was shameful in my eyes. I slowly let go of the church from that point on because I was disgusted that people knew what had happened. It's funny how when people in church know your business they all of a sudden begin to care a little more. Or so it seems.

Be careful to discern who actually is invested in your life to see you grow and who is just digging for information so they have something to talk about.

My parents had told every soul they knew that walked the grounds of this church. With good intentions they reached out to the members, but in my eyes it was pure shame. And in my eyes, from that point forward when anyone would reach out to me I believed it was because they felt bad for me. Which in many cases, were true. Showing my face was appalling because I knew that everyone knew what was going on. What was even worse was some of the people at the church were great people who I looked up to. So to see them after all that was happening was hurtful because I didn't understand the concept of grace. I didn't understand that some people there were not there to criticize me, but in fact, they were people who God specifically placed there to show love. But when we're in sin, we are so blinded to the truth. And we are blinded to grace.

I didn't have many passions but I began to hate church with a passion. I didn't believe anything anybody said because it seemed as if people only reached out when it was convenient for them. People would be kind to my face but then talk poorly when I wasn't around. Which I'll be very honest and be the first to own up and say this is the case in many churches today. Let's do better. Let's not invite people to hate Jesus because of how we act when we call ourselves Christians.

Knowing Jesus now, my view on the church is entirely different. I don't go to church because all the people there are so incredible. Not at all. Church people can be some of the worst people. I go to church because I know Jesus, and I love him. I go to church because I will admit that a lot of church attendees and even church staff are not the most kind. I go because instead of sitting back saying how someone needs to help shift culture — I can put my foot forward and try myself before asking someone else to.

Knowing Jesus now, I see the blood. And in each drip that falls onto the ground of humankind, I see every murder. I see the faces of the wrongdoers. I see the faces of the backstabbers. Of the gossipers. Of the bullies. And in them, I see all of us. I see sacred red drops and I see every deceptive lie. I see every aching torment and I see every empty bottle. But in it all, I see an overwhelming calm and a preordained triumph. I look at this man on the rugged cross and in agony there is perfect commitment.

With every ounce of effort I watch him open his eyes to see the backs of the ones that are walking away. I watch Him turn his head to the ones who were holding the sticks and watch His face ponder for the ones who have never seen Him. And in desperation I hear the question from the crowd over and over,

"Are they still worth it?"

In the wretchedness there is this glory.
In the ache there is this hallowed redemption.
And in a paralyzing irony, I see this calamity now marked as holy.
And as human hesitation was silenced, the words that didn't even have to be spoken,

"They will always be worth it" would now fill up every empty space for the rest of eternity.

I don't go to church because everything is perfect inside the four walls. I go because this is the Jesus I know, and I want people to know this man through my actions of showing up honest.

I'M SORRY IF YOU HATE JESUS BECAUSE OF ME

"People may hate us because of Jesus. But they should never hate Jesus because of us."

Sometimes, people suck. Honestly. We all do. And some days, it's extremely hard to walk into a church sanctuary and say "Hi, this is me. Take it or leave it." Because unfortunately, a lot of people will take one look and choose to leave it and push you to the side. And as humans with hearts that were made breakable - We have to remember that the people who leave are people with their own insecurities, too. That the people who leave, are still people who need love and acceptance, too. I don't know why us humans are the way that we are sometimes. We can be so cruel and we can be so selfish. And we can be so big-headed with eyes only for our own well being. Even people who shout to the rooftops of how important church is to them, I know. And this is a girl who has seen it and is apologizing for that.

I get it. Not everyone is going to stand tall behind this Jesus guy we all talk about. And like that quote, some people may hate us because of Jesus. And that's totally fine. But they should never hate Jesus because of us. There's a lot of people reading this who probably feel some type of way about Christianity because of a way they saw someone act who proclaimed to be a christian. Whether that be someone saying one thing and living out another, whether that be someone living in a religious bubble or someone living a little too freely (If ya know what I mean). Regardless, nobody should ever hate Jesus because of us. And if that is the case, I am so sorry.

I'm sorry for the person who cursed you out but then posted about worship on their social media story the same day. I'm sorry for the person who invited everyone to the party except for you but then talked about how Jesus loves unity. I'm sorry for the person who got black out drunk with you but then was greeting at church the next morning. I'm sorry for the person who talked about you behind your back but was preaching a message the next week. I'm sorry for the person who told you Jesus was mad at you for that one mistake. I'm sorry for the person who abused you but said it was okay because Jesus would forgive them. I'm sorry for the person who said you have to be perfect for someone to love you. I'm sorry for the person who represented Jesus so poorly to you.

Now, before somebody gets offended hear me out. For the people who have acted out of emotion and got back up, that's different. There is grace for that because we're all human. I sure as heck have had my fair share of making stupid decisions and acting out of spite that ultimately hurt other people. I have had my fair share of running in circles and repeating cycles. But, I'm talking about when we use Jesus as a cop out to our own actions. When we continue living however we want to but justify it because, "Jesus forgives." What we so quickly look over is that whether we like it or not, people ARE watching us. And people ARE watching how we act, how we react, and how we respond. There is a weight that comes with proclaiming that we are disciple of Christ.

If no one has ever told you, let me tell you that it matters when you're in bed with somebody on a Saturday and show up on Sunday with absolutely no remorse. It does matter. It maters when you're rude to that waitress or waiter but then you're sweet as can be when someone important is around. It does matter. It matters when you judge people for how they're living but then you're living the exact same way behind closed doors. It does matter. It matters when you exclude the people who are known as the "outcast". It matters when you only care about the people who can help get you somewhere. It does matter. As christians, and as decent human beings, but especially christians - we need to own who we are and we need to cheer on people for who they are. That's what Jesus did.

Big and bold.
Soft and quiet.
Awkward and clumsy.
Funny and serious.
Athletic and artistic.
Black and white.
Human and human.

When we set aside our pride and our preconceptions of being too much or not being enough, we'll start to see the really good stuff about us AND the really good stuff about other people, too. No masks and no trying to put on things that will never fit us. Just showing up as we are being exactly that. And welcoming in people who are exactly that, too. That's what Jesus did. He welcomed everyone and was kind to everyone. He walked out what he preached because he had the sweet understanding that there were eyes that were watching him. Wanted or not, there were always eyes. We can get so caught up in striving to be a certain way. In striving to be different and striving to be unique. wW get so obsessed in wanting to live right or so obsessed in living in our individuality that we miss the whole point.

I think we will be the different we are trying to achieve when our focus shifts from trying to be different to trying to be more like Jesus.

Here's the thing. In the end, we are not going to remember how cool that group of popular people thought we were. And in the end, Jesus is not going to look us in the eyes and applaud us for the way we conformed ourselves to fit in with them either. Likewise, He is not going to applaud us for pushing the outcasts aside in pursuit of attaining something for our own glory. I think there comes a point in all of our lives where the Lord stops us in our tracks and shows us who we are. Because sometimes, praise God for this, it takes our world falling apart to obtain the realization that this isn't our world after all. That this isn't about us after all. It's about Him. And it's our job to love people so dang well that they're only response is, "If this is how Jesus is… then I'm in."

FILLING SPACES

At fourteen, I felt like humanity hated me. So naturally, I began to hate them, too. I was drowning in condemnation, but looking back it was all in my head. Because never once did anyone shame me other than myself. Which if many of us look back, that seems to be the case for a lot of us. I was in a very lonely season at the time in my life. I had the boyfriend, but at a distance and in secret. I was in church every Sunday and Wednesday, but my mom paid me to be. Just because you are in church does not mean anything. Which is why I'm a firm believer on noticing the fruit of someone's life and not just their words or even presence. The happy about life girl had disappeared and I didn't recognize who I was becoming to be. At fourteen, marijuana became my only friend, alcohol became my escape, and that boy became my identity.

Us humans do a really good job at treating the things we think we want as a missing piece while we quickly lend our persistence a hammer to slam it in so that what we want can fit our puzzle. But what a sorry way to live — filling our space with things we want but were never meant to have. Letting our selfish eagerness tamper with what was suppose to come in due time. If we would take a step back, I think we'd all see that a half empty puzzle makes more sense than a crammed full puzzle that doesn't create the picture it was suppose to. We have to know who we are before we pick up a piece to add in our puzzle. Because when we know who we are, we know what will fit. When we know who we are, we have the deeper understanding how every piece effects every other piece.

And through adding pieces and picking the pushed ones out — we'll learn that empty space feels more full than it ever did even when it was filled with wrong pieces. I really believe, in an odd kind of way, feeling full with the empty is better than feeling vacant in the full.

It's tough when we create who we are in another person who is not Jesus. Because when we identify ourselves with a human being, when that person is not with us, we are no longer with us either. Without that boyfriend, I never felt whole. And it's ironic, because looking back I see now that even with him, I was never once whole. And that's exactly what it is. Sin has this unruly way of wrapping itself around our neck and blurring our vision. In the moment, it's all fun and games. In the moment, these things that fill us up seem like it's all we have. But eventually, we will obtain the deep recognition that it was actually robbing and destroying more pieces of our soul than filling spaces in our soul like we thought.

I hope that I am opening the door for you to know how I genuinely felt in each moment. I have a read many books of stories, but they were merely stories. In my story, I want to get down to the core, and let you in a little bit more than what is classified as acceptable. I want the option for people to know how I felt without trying to make it pretty. I want my really human failures to be raw. Because I may be in a more steady place now, but I wasn't always here. I want the hearts that read this to feel my humanness all the way through.

It was November, and there I was maneuvering the alarm system at my house so I could sneak out and sneak people in. Bringing the boys in, or going out with the boys. Truly, I don't know what happened to me. I was a completely different person who had no fear of punishment because I wanted to do what I wanted to do. I had no respect for rules. I made fun of Christians. I would make jokes of my spot in hell that I was on my way towards. I was not sober. I was dark, and heavy. I am nothing less than baffled looking back to all of my stories because they are all not what a fifteen year old girl should have at that point.

I know a lot of us never expected in our wildest dreams to be in the situations we have found ourselves in before. Some situations caused by our own decisions, some situations caused by others. Maybe some caused by both. Maybe as humans, let's not be too hard on ourselves and forget that we are in fact human. We have to mess up so that God can show himself to us later on in a way that he never could have shown us on the mountain top. Maybe we had to trip back there and fall flat on our face so that now we can feel God in a way we never could have felt standing tall. Maybe we had to have gone empty handed sometimes so that now we are able to pick up what he has waiting for us.

Perhaps, maybe, everything we did terribly wrong was the footing for everything God intended to do overwhelmingly right. And in a holy paradox, that's exactly it.

For the one who feels like your feet can never find solid ground to stand on, it's okay. For the one who is trying to tip toe through their existence because no one sees you anyways, we see you, and we love you. For the one who everyone always thought was whack because you've had dreams that were wildly impossible to the human eye, that's more than okay. And for the one who blinks really fast and starts to shrink back at the mere thought of success, you are just as capable as anybody else is. I will tell you, there are going to be times when we are more than people prefer us to be. Too honest. Too loud. Too ambitious. Too sure. Too broken. Too complicated. Too awake for our brokenness. And because of that, I think that's why it's easy to walk into a room and conform to whoever is around us.

But I don't believe our story is deserving to be conformed.

I don't believe our integrity is deserving to be shoved to the side so that it can run after the approval of culture. I don't believe it's okay to seep into the normality of planning our every move to fit a non-existent mold. I don't believe we exist to be someone who we craft together from a million different pieces from a million different people around us. We are all different yet we are all really good at being a tourist in each others skin. Sometimes it takes sinking. Sometimes it takes stepping over the shattered pieces of your old self. Sometimes it takes really big leaps onto new territory all before you seem to find a ground that isn't cold. Sometimes it takes dreaming. Please, please, please dream. Dream bigger than yourself and let God rock your socks off, because He will. Sure thing. We are all different and we are all in different seasons. Life is always hitting us with change and we are always changing. But I learned that even so, God is our biggest fan in every single season.

You aren't in this by yourself.

HONEST TRUTH

"Because of this decision we don't evaluate people by what they have or how they look. We looked at the Messiah that way once and got it all wrong, as you know. We certainly don't look at him that way anymore. Now we look inside, and what we see is that anyone united with the Messiah gets a fresh start, is created new. The old life is gone; a new life burgeons! Look at it! All this comes from the God who settled the relationship between us and him, and then called us to settle our relationships with each other. God put the world square with himself through the Messiah, giving the world a fresh start by offering forgiveness of sins. God has given us the task of telling everyone what he is doing. We're Christ's representatives. God uses us to persuade men and women to drop their differences and enter into God's work of making things right between them. We're speaking for Christ himself now: Become friends with God; he's already a friend with you."

2 Corinthians 5:17-20 (MSG)

CHALLENGE

Just because everyone can be genuine, doesn't mean everyone is genuine. And just because you want to be everybody's number one fan, doesn't mean you should be. In my own life, I have chased more than what I was capable of and I have made rooms in my heart to seat many people who never stayed for coffee, only for a short meal. Often, we think about all the feet that have walked out of the rooms in our heart and we catch ourselves keeping count of how many times we heard the door shut one by one. But what I have learned, slowly, is that it doesn't matter who's walked out of the room. The predominant prize is who still is in the room.

Not everyone is genuine, so be careful with who you rearrange your space for. Yes, I'm a BIG believer in there being good in every soul. But you can't bring people close holding onto the expectation of the authenticity you believe to see in them. You, yourself, be kind. Welcome everyone with a smile but not everyone with a seat. You can still believe the best while standing wise.

REFLECTION

I.   How do you determine who actually is invested in your life to see you grow and who is just digging for information so they have something to talk about? How do you deal with the people who are just seeming to dig for information?

II. Have you ever believed that other people were looking at you in condemnation and judgement when really, you were the only person who was shaming yourself? How did you move forward? How do you differentiate conviction and condemnation?

III. What season have you had to walk empty handed in so you were able to pick up what God had waiting for you? What did you learn?

IV. Have you rearranged your space for people that you maybe shouldn't have? What prompted you to do so? What did you learn from it?

The Second Table

CHAPTER 4

WHO AM I

There I was, fifteen and standing on feeble falsehood that I can handle my mess. I had a few close friends, not many. I will never forget laying in my bed one afternoon as I heard my mom coming down the stairs, she hardly ever came downstairs. I remember her pushing my door open in fury asking if I had been sleeping around. I gave her a blank stare in utter shock that she had even asked me that. I sat up stunned. I didn't even try to lie (that was a first). I owned up to it and it proceeded into a big argument.

I told her I didn't need her and how I know what I'm doing. Because duh, when we're fifteen we definitely have it all together. Everyone knows that. (Lord, help us). I was hateful and I was aware of it. I remember being so upset because in my mind, I was convinced I wasn't doing anything wrong. I was just trying to feel something in a soul that was numb and it seemed as if no one understood that. And you know what we call that? Justification. And you know what I learned years later? If we have to trip over our feet to try and justify something we are doing, we shouldn't be doing it in the first place. End of discussion.

Justification is simply an invitation to a compromised lifestyle.

Unaware of what justification meant, I really believed no one understood without the affection from that boy, because of how emotionally abusive the relationship was I honestly didn't know how to function. I would get physically sick and not eat for days. Or even more so, I feel like the girls who are going through this in their own lives feel as if no one understands their severity of it. But I want to tell you, that I too, have been there.

In the back of my mind, I hated how I disappointed my mom. I really did. And I couldn't bare the thought of how much I hurt my dad so it was easier for me to sweep it all under the carpet and continue to do what I was doing. I didn't see a way out, so I dug deeper each time I messed up. You ever been there? You feel like you've dropped the ball way too hard and it's easier to keep doing what you're doing than it is to own up and get right? It's hard. I know it. But I'm thankful for a God who doesn't drop us when we drop the ball. I'm thankful for a God who keeps us when we don't keep ourselves.

I remember the weeks that I would spend in bed listening to the silence, with no motivation for anything. I lost all hope in every area. I heard over and over how much potential I had for all of these great things but I didn't care. It didn't make sense to me.

WHAT DOES POTENTIAL MEAN?

"Potential — Having or showing the capacity to become or develop into something in the future."

I wish that someone would have called out the good things they saw in me at that specific time and dropped the whole "potential" phrase. I wish that someone would have spoke to the greatness that was inside of me already, not this greatness that I could achieve one day if I tried to. I wish that someone would have brought to light the promise on my life and not the hopeful potential of what could be.

Potential of what someone could be does not mean anything to somebody who is contemplating their life in the moment. If anything, that idea of potential gives more of an incentive to take the easy way out because it seems so unattainable. Speaking life to somebody of who they could be one day is necessary, yes. However, speaking life to somebody of who they are in that moment is crucial.

Up until my freshman year of High School, I usually never made a grade lower than a B. Freshman year, I never made anything higher than a D. My mind wasn't present at school, it was always distressed. Days on days were spent of me crying to whatever this higher power was for some kind of escape from my own emotions. Years back, I found a journal page from when I was fifteen. I had written, "Every thought is a vicious battle and every breath is an un-ending war. And I don't think I'm winning anymore."

I know authentic, deep-rooted pain. The kind that stings your innermost being. And I believe you have known it, too. That's why you're still reading. And let me tell you, if I made it, you're going to make it, too.

TO THE ONE WHO FEELS LIKE NO ONE UNDERSTANDS

Hey, you.

If you're reading this then please know you can trust what I'm about to tell you. I get it. Trust seems like a foreign word, but the fact that you are reading this tells me that there is something in you that is searching. Searching for an answer, searching for a way out, searching for healing. Searching for something tangible. I do not want to tell you I am sorry that things have turned out the way they have. I'm almost certain there has been enough people to tell you that. But I am sorry, I am so sorry your heart feels like it can't ever be mended. Gosh, it's hard to move throughout the day when your heart feels like it's under rocks too heavy for you to pick up. I know at times, it really is unbearable. At times, it really does take every ounce of effort to get a deep breath in.

But can I tell you that six months from now your life is not going to look how it looks now. Six months from now you're going to be sitting still somewhere and everything is going to be different. I don't promise many things, but this I stand tall behind. One day you're going to take a step back and you're going to stand there and see where everything fell into place. You won't even have a single clue how it did. There will be day where everything you see begins to look back at you differently. And in some whimsical way, it'll make sense. Don't you dare give up now. Don't you dare believe that this ache isn't worth it. Don't you dare let life steal your shout. When life tries to steal your shout, shout louder. When the enemy is trying to steal your joy, praise bigger. When your mind is trying to tell you you're not worth it, tell your mind that God is worth it. You're going to make it. You're going to come out on top. You're going to have your story completed.

Love,
A Broken Fifteen Year Old Who Wish Someone Told Her This

Freshman year. Sixth period. Gym class. If you have been in a High School you know the gym leads to the field and parking outside, and fitting enough the girls locker room was right next to the door. The boyfriend had a baseball game he wanted me to go to, but it was during school hours and there was no way my parents were going to let me miss school for him. They were unaware we were still seeing each other.

However, it worked out so the time that he had to leave to get there, was the same time I was going to be in gym class. Which meant I could easily slide out the doors when the bell rang. Although, if I snuck out then I would miss seventh period and the school would call my parents and inform them that I wasn't present. But complication never stopped me. We had this planned a few days in advanced so a couple days beforehand I went to the front office at my school and handed them a piece of paper. I had written down that my parents had gotten a new number and I wrote down my number in place of theirs.

So when I missed class, the school called me instead of them. (Smart decisions with Hope part eight, maybe?) The day came and the girls all were in the locker room changing and I received the text that him and his friend were there and that there wasn't anybody around so I was clear to go. The bell rang and in hesitation, I darted out those doors as fast as I could and hopped in the car. We all laughed as we drove away while I told my parents I was going to my friend Caitlyn's house after school. As slick as I thought I was, my parents were not stupid.

Angrily, they showed up to Caitlyn's house and the mom told them that I was never there. So when I got home they were not happy and automatically accused me of being with him. They were most definitely right. However, I threw a fit about how they never trust me and how I was at a soccer game with my friend, Justin. I proceeded to tell them the reason I didn't tell them was because I didn't think they would let me go since it was with a guy. Directly after that I called my friend Justin and told him the story and asked him to cover for me.

Justin called my dad and told him how I was with him at the soccer game and surprisingly, I got off the hook. I know what you're thinking, "Oh my gosh, what was wrong with this girl." Yep. No clue. I was lost and I was a compulsive liar, too. 2013 was spent lying and believing that abuse in a relationship is normal. That possessiveness means love. And that sexual affection is what fixed problems.

MY PARENTS TOOK MY BEDROOM DOOR

It started with a Youth Conference of over 12,000 students that is every June through the church my parents moved us to. My dad didn't allow me to go to the conference because the boyfriend was going to be going. Instead, I sat in my room alone because I didn't have any friends other than him. Totally normal, right? Mhm. Not quite. At the end of each night of the conference, the boyfriend would come through my window and stay the night in my house.

Well, get this. On the last day of the conference, he was at the mall with his friends and they just so happened to run into one of my mothers friends. I was sitting in my room later that day and my mom called me to come upstairs because she had to have a talk with me. She proceeded to tell me how this boy never loved me and how he had me fooled because her friend ran into him at the mall and he had hickeys all over his neck. I sat in silence for a good ten minutes and let her continue to talk about how she was right while I contemplated in my head the two directions this conversation could go. I could tell her she was right, and avoid her finding out he was staying in the house with me. Or, I could let my pride shut it down and tell her they were from me.

"You're wrong. They're actually from me."

I blurted out quicker than I could think as I watched the shock sit down on her face and felt my eyes widen bigger than my head. After I said that I instantly regretted it because I knew she was going to tell my dad and now, that was just awkward. Long story short, I ended up watching my brother and my father carry my mattress upstairs into the dining room. (My brother had recently moved back home after completing his program). And then I stood and watched as my dad unscrewed the nails on my bedroom and bathroom doors and watched as he took them down and put them in the garage.

My new bedroom was the dining room and I was not able to even go downstairs to the restroom unless someone walked me down there and waited outside the room for me. I can't make this stuff up. Y'all, I slept on a mattress in my dining room for weeks and my walls were moving boxes. That first night when I was laying on my bed in the dining room, I was so broken. I think in that moment I was realizing how downhill my life had gone, and I didn't know what to do. That night was the night where I couldn't juggle my pain and poor decisions anymore. I was growing to a point where I began to hate myself and the mess I was in.

I made my way downstairs and I don't know if any of you have been in a position of pain like this, but my body was so frail I could hardly walk from crying in desperation. And so I crawled into my into my bathroom, laid in fetal position and sobbed until I was vomiting. That was the night I found satisfaction in self harm. Because when I physically caused myself pain, it demanded all of my attention and for a split second, it was like a breath of fresh air. Because all of the inward pain subsided, and my attention was brought to minimal physical pain. And that was a lot easier to deal with than the human soul.

The next morning I rode in the car for eight hours with hardly any words spoken. My parents were taking me to Florida. Shame. Shame was suffocating me and my little mind did not have the first clue how to handle it so when we got to the hotel, the first thing I did was steal my mothers razor in the bathroom and relieve myself the only way I knew how. I remember that week I bought a sweatshirt and I wore it everyday in the blazing sun. Because God forbid my parents find out about that, too. That trip was so very awkward and I just cried. A lot. Because I knew they were going to move me down there away from what I knew in Georgia. Any parent knows their child. They could see how drained and broken I was when we got back from the trip and they actually offered to let me have my friends from where I use to live come visit for a day. Now, through being rebellious and sneaking out and sneaking people in, through drinking and giving myself away, through self harm, there was still more. Because when we are caught in a cycle of repetitive sin, it never just stays in one lane. Sin is expansive. Sin does not maintain itself in only one specific area. Sin owns one specific area then moves its way to another. Then before we know it, sin can rule the entirety of our lives.

Just as an Earthly parent knows their child, God is the same way. But He's deeper. In our mess, He's further than we are. In the frustration, He's slowing us down to see a glimpse of Him. He's good. I don't know where you've been, but He's good. I don't know who does not understand, but He's good. And you need to get that in your soul. He is good. He is good. He is good.

> *"Why are you cast down, O my soul,*
> *and why are you in turmoil within me?*
> *Hope in God; for I shall again praise him,*
> *my salvation and my God. "*
> *Psalm 42:5-6 (ESV)*

In Psalm 42 and 43, you'll read this passage three times. Three representing what is solid, real, and substantial. David writes "Why are you cast down, o my soul, and why are you in turmoil within me?" Then directly after he writes "Hope in God; for I shall again praise him. My salvation and my God." I adore these passages because it's been so prevalent in our lives. All of us. David speaks to his soul (his mind, will, and emotions) and is asking in desperation "Why are you down cast?" Because his heart is for God and his spirit is well, but yet his soul is faint. So he speaks to it while regaining sight of what he knows "Hope in God; I shall again praise him."

He's good. Disregarding whatever life is throwing at you, take heart because you SHALL again praise him.

FRUIT SHOWS WHAT WORDS CANNOT

First and foremost, I want to tell you that it's totally okay for wanting to be in a relationship. That doesn't mean you're desperate, it means you're human and you recognize your natural breathed desire for human affection. And on the flip side, it's totally okay for not wanting anything right now. That doesn't mean you're hypercritical, it means you're learning deeper parts of who you are and in the right time someone is going to appreciate that. More than anything, dating is so exaggerated. There's been this unspoken timeline of when you should start dating, when you should be engaged, and when you should be married considering kids. And it's all whack haha. Just because your life may not reflect the image you had of what your life was going to look like at whatever age you may be does NOT mean you have done something wrong.

Just because your ten-step plan of your future isn't happening on the timeline you created does NOT mean God is not in it. Just because you still have emotions over past relationships does NOT mean someone else isn't going to come along and you are meant to go back to your old relationship. It just means you're really human and you have really human emotions as we all do.

I say it all the time, but we're all human. Pain is so inevitable. Especially when you are putting your heart, the most vulnerable and fragile piece we hold, on the line with another human. If you think about it, that just sounds like a disaster. But my friend, here's the thing. I have learned to thank God for allowing other people to hurt me. I know, now I'm the one who sounds whack. But really, there have been times in my life where I have tried to run back to doors God intentionally shut. And in my own humanness, I would stay and try to pry those doors back open. But I learned that because God is a caring God who has my best interest, He would allow specific people to deeply wound my heart. All for the purpose to widen my eyes with the realization and recognition of what I do not want. And more importantly, what I do not need. And that's the thing about pain.

Pain does not happen to destroy us. Pain actually happens to reconstruct us.

There are so many different stages in life and personally, I believe stages of life play a big part in determining if you are even at a healthy place to start pursuing a relationship. Notice how I say pursue a relationship and not look for a relationship. The moment you find yourself in a frantic search for a relationship is the moment you need to be wise enough to step back. Really, chill out. The God that has been so faithful to you this whole time is more than capable in this area. The last thing you want to do is create something with your own human hands. Because if create something with your hands, then you have to maintain it with your hands. It just doesn't work. Because the Lord is so gracious, He will only allow you to hold onto something your hands are not meant to carry for so long until He ends it.

A lot of people have this false understanding that after you dedicate your life to the Lord then you're automatically ready for this redeemed godly relationship. My friend, that is not the case. Let me provide some clarity. The first step in Christianity is salvation. We all know that. Your second step is not this big youth pastor role. Your second step is not this creative arts director. Your second step is not to launch your dream business. Your second step is not to be a husband or a wife.

Your second step, biblically, is sanctification. I know, I know this sounds a little too wordy and religious. But hear me out. After saying yes to Jesus, your next step is committing yourself and dedicating yourself into becoming more like Christ. In really taking a step to the side and digging into who you are, what needs to be worked out, what needs to be planted to grow, what needs to be sharpened. It's a process. And if you jump into a relationship before taking that time, you are not going to be the person you need to be for that relationship. Being content in singleness is not learning to accept that if God never brings you a spouse then you'll be okay. I think that's extreme. If it's your heart's desire to be married one day, the Lord knows that.

Being content in singleness is walking in the willingness of allowing God to shed light on areas that still need redemption. Being content in singleness is pressing pause to understand the heart of God a little bit more knowing that it's good for you, and for the one who you'll be with one day.

Okay, so I touched on a few things for us to personally be aware of when it comes to relationships. But what about things to look for in the other person? That's a big one that has many different opinions. In my opinion, and based off my experiences, these are some key components that have changed my life and outlook on this whole thing.

1   **There is a difference between someone who knows God and someone who is in love with God.**

Ask the deep questions. Ask who Jesus is to them. Watch how they respond in worship. Listen to them tell their story. Are they passionate about their relationship? Or is it just the casual, "I got saved when I was eight and have been a Christian ever since." Are they passionate about conversations that dig deeper? Can you even hold conversation about these things?

2   **Don't enter into a relationship with a person who does not show fruit of the characteristics you desire in a partner.**

As someone who will always look to find the best in people, this one is tough. Because if you're anything like me then it's easy for you to look past issues and see people for who they can be one day. But when it comes to a relationship, you have to see things black and white. If you don't want a partner who drinks, then don't step into a relationship with someone who goes out clubbing just because they told you they'll stop. If you don't want a partner who is possessive, then don't step into a relationship with someone who consistently questions where you're at and what you're doing just because they said they'll work on it. Because sure. If someone cares about you, they'll stop these habits. But my friend, that is shaky ground. I have seen this firsthand and fresh. When you enter into a relationship with someone who conforms into the characteristics that you desire, you will realize that is not really who you are pursuing a relationship with. That is merely the person you have almost created them to be. It's sad, but it's true. And nine times out of ten, the moment that relationship ends they will run right back to what they left when you met them. Because their change was not birthed out of a place of authenticity. Look for someone who has a consistent pattern of walking with characteristics you desire. Fruit says what words cannot.

3   As a girl, if you are the one who has to set the sexual bound-aries in a relationship – run.

I don't care how hot they are. How good of a person they are. How kind they are. How much potential they may have. If a lady is the one who is having to step back and have the hard conversation of boundaries the relationship needs, you are in for an exhausting road of feeling as if you are leading the relationship. As a lady, if a man cannot set up the boundaries and control to keep the relationship holy, then you need to evaluate where the relationship is headed in all areas.

If you're dating with a purpose to lead to marriage, then these kind of conversations and decisions are necessary for the man to be able to make. A lady needs to be confident that the man is spiritually mature to know where he stands. But same for the ladies, if you expect the man to pursue purity, you need to as well. This is not a double standard debate.

4   Watch how they act and respond around their friends.

You really get a deeper insight to who someone is when you see them around their friends. When they're with their friends, there's no guard up and there's no filter. If they don't cuss around you, but are throwing F bombs around their friends – notice it. If they don't drink around you, but have no problem going out with their friends – notice it. These little things speak loudly.

5   If there's an unwavering uncertainty – don't ignore it.

My friend, your intuition goes a long way. When you're with the right person it's supposed to be easy. Yes, there will be hard conversations and bumps in the road. But if you're walking with uncertainty, pay attention to it. And be brave enough to walk away. Regardless of where you are in life, what position you hold, who is watching – it is NEVER too late to listen to your heart and walk away. I promise you. Don't try to figure it out and don't try to ignore it. Something that really got me was this. When you say yes to Jesus, you say yes to peace. Peace is not something you have to go and search for. What do you mean? Because peace is a subcomponent of Christianity. So, you never have to go and "seek out peace". You walk in peace when you walk with Jesus. It's the moment you notice you don't have that peace… When you realize that you lost it, that's when you know.

I say all of this to say it matters who you invest your time into. Don't dwell on the past. And don't think you're still tied down to your past just because it pops up from time to time. I'm full time in ministry and I know God. But I know my human memories, too. I know God but I know my human experiences, too. I know God but I know my human heart, too. Take your experiences and count them as learning material. I don't know everything, but I have certainly learned a whole lot and I hope this meant something to you. When your attention is on Him, He will exceed your expectations. Every time. And it will never be how you imagined it would be. And that's the beauty of it. Be true to you. Don't compromise. And when the time comes, love with all you have.

HONEST TRUTH

"For it is you who light my lamp;

the Lord my God lightens my darkness.

For by you I can run against a troop,

and by my God I can leap over a wall.

This God—his way is perfect;[d]

the word of the Lord proves true;

he is a shield for all those who take refuge in him.

For who is God, but the Lord?

And who is a rock, except our God?—

the God who equipped me with strength

and made my way blameless.

He made my feet like the feet of a deer

and set me secure on the heights.

He trains my hands for war,

so that my arms can bend a bow of bronze.

You have given me the shield of your salvation,

and your right hand supported me,

and your gentleness made me great.

You gave a wide place for my steps under me,

and my feet did not slip.

I pursued my enemies and overtook them,

and did not turn back till they were consumed.

I thrust them through, so that they were not able to rise;

they fell under my feet.

For you equipped me with strength for the battle;

you made those who rise against me sink under me."

Psalm 18:28-39 (ESV)

CHALLENGE

More than anything in my life I am certain that the One who breathes life into our own lungs, will never allow us to be in pain for no reason. He does not cross his arms when we are reaching out. He does not close His eyes on our frailty. He does not hide when we are distraught. And He does not turn His back on our instability. But He's the kind of God who gets down and says, "Hey, come closer. Let me show you how we're gonna use this." This week, reach out to someone who has been going through a difficult time. Rather than encouraging them with who they could be one day, dig a little deeper and point out some really good things about them. Help them to feel noticed and that they have positive gifts about them now.

REFLECTION

I.   Have you ever been in a season where you kept digging deeper each time you messed up? Why do you think you kept digging rather than putting a stop to whatever it was you were doing?

I.   What does the phrase, "You have so much potential" mean to you? Is there anyone in your life you need to pull out the current strengths instead of pointing out their future potential?

II.   What kind of situations in your past have you been in that you feel like no one else would understand? How have you used these situations to relate with others? What can you obtain from these situations to impact somebody else?

III.   I believed abuse in a relationship is normal. That possessiveness meant love. And that sexual affection is what fixed problems. Can you relate to any of these? If yes, how did your views on these change? If no, what are some false things you have believed?

IV.   Like David spoke to his soul to regain sight of who God was - What in your life do you need to speak to?

The Second Table

CHAPTER 5

THANK GOD FOR WHAT DIDN'T HAPPEN

I was a big fan of free stuff. Shoplifting was my secondary hobby. I had been involved in this for a few months when my friends made their way up to see me in Gainesville. So guess what we decided to do when they got here? Casually go to the mall. For a long while, I looked at this situation in black and white as if I wasn't in the wrong. But just as a big portion of my life, I was very much in the wrong. We were in a popular department store and I was doing my thing. I had my shopping bag from another store and I was grabbing what I wanted into my bag.

We were walking out of the store and all of a sudden were stopped by a sherif asking us to come with him. My heart completely dropped because I knew this was going to drive my parents up a wall. Once again, I was mad about the outcome rather than being mad about what got me there in the first place. Dangerous. The sheriff walked us to the back room in the security office and I sat and listened as the sherif called my mother and told her he was waiting for her to come take a seat because we were caught shoplifting.

I looked up as my mom stormed in while disbelief was painted firm on her face. I didn't even care at this point that I was disappointing my parents, I was at the point where I had no remorse for my actions anymore. My mom was talking about how this was way over the line and I remember just snapping on her in that moment. I accepted the fact this was who I was and I wasn't getting better, and I just wanted her to accept it, too. I laid down on my bed in my dining room (LOL) and waited till about midnight to softly tip toe down to the basement into my old room. Although they had moved me upstairs, I still had my windows tampered in a way where they could be open and closed with the alarm system set.

And so I lifted up the window as quietly as I could, and I went to a party that night that was happening in my neighborhood. In my head, I was already in a ditch that I wasn't getting out of so I had nothing to lose. I stumbled back to my window early that morning and fumbled my way back inside. In my intoxicated head I tip toed back up the stairs but realistically, I probably stomped. But I made it to the dining room, and I laid there awake all night. I felt as if my world was completely ending. I felt hopeless. Useless. Like I was never going to see light. That night was longer than others. I tossed and turned and was so unsettled. It was early, way earlier than I ever got up and I heard my parents on the back porch. Groggy eyed, I got up to see what they were saying because my name was being said repetitively. They motioned for me to come out and something seemed stiff, and the atmosphere was muggy. We sat in silence on the old wooden chairs while I could feel them examining my countenance. I could tell they knew I wasn't in the right state of mind.

My dad begin to tell me how they had reserved a bed for me at an all woman's Christian rehabilitation program for addicts. I could feel as my insides lit on fire and my hands turned into fists. I didn't feel sad, I was angry. This program they were sending me to was the same program my brother went through, but for girls. It was intense. It was brutal. It was secluded. My parents continued to talk about how this was my only option and there was no way around it, and we were leaving next Monday. I sat in fury and finally when I spoke, I blurted out how I was going to kill myself if they sent me there.

The scary thing is, I was not bluffing when I said that. And I had thought about it before, but never had I said it out loud. I was already planning it out in my head because if they sent me there I would have been in a place where the Bible would be shoved down my throat. And because of church hurt I was at a place in my life where I quite literally would have rather die than to have this Jesus person try and come in my life. There was not an amount of money in the world someone could have given me to proclaim this Jesus guy. Because I developed the belief that there was no belief. After I spoke my parents sat in disbelief. And I walked away in disbelief. How is this happening to me? Why am I the way that I am? Don't they see that if they would just let me go then everything would be okay? Don't they see that the more they try to help the worse I get? Why does no one understand? Why can't I understand? Why does every step hurt? All of these questions flooded my thoughts and I could never make them silent.

It was the end of July 2013. I was very unstable. I was at a loss. I was kicked out of youth group at my church. Who even gets kicked out of youth? This girl does. I spent each day laying in bed with no agenda. One day I sat down with my mom and bawled my eyes out. I was going in with a backup plan and I told her I knew I needed help but how I know I wouldn't last at the program. I was honestly just saying anything and everything that I could to make me sound as if I had remorse. I didn't, but I didn't want to go to that program. We came to the conclusion that I was going to commit to counseling at our church we were attending, and I did. She called almost immediately and had me scheduled in. I remember walking into my first session with one of the kind men who worked there, and I was incredibly rude. Didn't say a word to him through the whole hour.

I didn't want to talk to people about my feelings. I felt as if no one would understand. I tried to verbally relay my feelings to my parents and was always shut down. So why on Earth would I try with someone who I didn't even know? My parents sat me down and told me that there was one condition they would let the boyfriend and I be together again, and it was that if he went and completed the same rehabilitation program my brother had completed. We made an agreement if he completed the program they would allow us to get married and we could put an end to all of the craziness. We called him and had him come over to the house so we could talk about our options. To make a long story short from here, he went against his family and ended up agreeing to go to the program.

My mom and I packed all his things with him and we drove him down to the program the very next week. That time was bittersweet. My mom and I sure have had our disagreements, but she did quietly have my back in this season. Days later, I stood as my eyes scanned over all the people unloading our car and carrying the boyfriend's bags in. My soul was frail and it had gotten to the time where it was time for my mom and I to leave him there. We walked on the bumpy gravel road and I stood as my mom said her goodbyes to him. She gave me a minute with him and that lump in my throat was almost too much to bare. That was the last time I saw him for years. As a fifteen year old girl, I didn't realize how traumatic this was to my soul. The only person who served as a home in my life was abruptly removed from my life. As I said before, when you form your identity in another human being, when they leave, you leave too. And in that moment, I watched my entire life leave my life.

WHAT DIDN'T MADE ROOM FOR WHAT DID

In my twenties, I remember this one time I was in my living room with some friends and we were all talking about the crazy things that have been going on in our lives in that season. And without thinking, I blurted out and was like, "Man.. Can you imagine if God answered every prayer we prayed? …Do you know how many husbands I would have?!" *Inserts face palm emoji* Obviously kidding. I mean, kind of?

If God really did answer every one of my prayers, I would have married my fourth grade crush, Kyle. My sixth grade boyfriend, Christopher. My seventh grade first real relationship, unnamed. And some of the in-between from thirteen to today. Thank God for what didn't happen. Am I right or am I right? Which I said this as a total joke but really. What if God answered EVERY prayer we ever prayed? Every prayer that came from a selfish request. Every prayer that came out of emotion and desperation. Every prayer that was for something that seemed good at the moment. You know? Some of us would be in some deep trouble.

What about the prayers we prayed for things we really thought we needed? The prayers for the things we were so expectant for? What about the prayers that seemed right? That seemed good? That seemed necessary? When we see our prayers answered, we get so giddy. Rightfully so, because God is a sovereign God and He is a GOOD God. We are so quick to thank Him for all the things He allowed to happen and we are so quick to throw up our hallelujah for the people he brought into our lives. We are real good at thanking Him for what He has done, but we are real blinded to all of the things He didn't do.

I've said this many times, but honestly. More than any lesson I have learned, more than anything someone has taught me. More than anything — I have learned to thank God for what DIDN'T happen. What do you mean? If God gave us everything we thought we needed, I guarantee we wouldn't be where we are today. If God allowed the people we thought were good for us to stay in our lives for as long as we thought needed, I guarantee we wouldn't be who we are today. If God gave us every job we asked for, I guarantee that we wouldn't have had the connections he intended us to have today. We have to understand that everything God withheld from us is just as important, if not more important, than the things He did give us. Because what He withheld from us made room for what He intended for us.

In our own humanity we don't understand why things happen the way they do. We don't understand why that person walked out of our lives, or why God had US walk out of their lives. We don't understand why someone else got the promotion. We don't understand why our big plan fell through. We don't understand why we hurt the way we do sometimes. In our own humanness, when something isn't happening the way we really believe it's suppose to happen we automatically grasp hold of the idea that something is wrong with us or we are doing something wrong. When the person we had feelings for walks out with no explantation, we automatically examine ourselves to try and figure out why.

When the other person gets the job we were wanting, we automatically think we weren't good enough. When nothing is happening how we anticipated, we think we missed something. But what our human eyes cannot see is all of these things taking place was to clear up the spot for what God intended the entire time. And it's funny because so many us sit here today and we are so in awe of where God has taken us. We are so thankful for everything He's done and all the things He's completed. But we miss all of the things that didn't happen. When we really look back over our lives and begin to notice all the things He withheld, our praise get louder for the things He kept from us over the things He gave to us. Because all of these people, jobs, relationships, friendships that we believed were good for us — He had a different plan all along.

So really.. I don't know about you but my life is a whole lot of,

Thank you God for allowing that job to fall through.

Because it made space for the one you intended that I have now.

Thank you God for allowing me to walk out of that relationship.

Because it made space for me to ready for the right one you intended in your timing.

Thank you God for allowing that friend to cut ties.

Because it made space for me to have fruitful friendships and not draining ones.

Thank you God for allowing me to walk in the dark seasons longer than I wanted.

Because it made space in my heart for you to teach me what was necessary for the next season.

It's because of what DIDN'T happen that we could experience what DID happen. It's because of what DIDN'T happen that we could appreciate what DID happen. It's because of what DIDN'T happen that we could love what DID happen. It's because of what DIDN'T happen that we are who we are, today. And only a God wise enough as Him would be so witty to have our lives play out like this. Because in the piles of confusion and ache, we can all look back and see a holy depiction of grace in each step.

Let's start saying, thanks God, *for what didn't happen.*

USE YOUR ACHE

Being back home was somber. My bed was put back in my room so I had a bedroom again, which was pretty nice. But in all actuality, I started my sophomore year of High School alone. I was fifteen, severely depressed. I wouldn't eat, and I was in counseling every week. Everyone at school knew my situation and I think that kept people from wanting to talk to me. I was a mess and I'm sure people wanted to stay away from it. Because that is exactly what society teaches us. To run away from the messy rather than run towards the messy. I had a few friends at a distance but really only one friend who was close. She knew my entire situation and everything that was going on. She was really my only friend who I confided in deeply.

If there was anyone I could count on, it was her. I was at school for about a month when my parents pulled me out. It was the second week of September when they told me we were moving to Florida. Everything I knew was here and we had moved a lot, yes. But we had never moved out of state. We packed up all of our things and two days before my sixteenth birthday, mom and I were driving all we had to Florida. I don't mention my dad a lot in this season of my life, because there wasn't much of a relationship there. In my mind he was not on my side and he took away the only thing that mattered to me. In my mind he didn't care about me.

Years later I never imagined that my dad would become my very best friend. I have never known restoration as I have with my dad and I. But in this season, it was me against everybody. And I was losing miserably. So there I was with mom, leaving it all behind. Although, I had nothing I was leaving except for broken relationships, hurtful memories, and a bad taste to my name. Gainesville, Georgia was a place that I would never move back to again.

We drove and drove and ended up in Sarasota, Florida. We lived in a hotel for a few weeks till we found a house. Two days after my birthday, mom and I were at dinner. She received a call from the program and it was the boyfriend. He told her that he was leaving the program. Mom handed me the phone and I heard the same empty words, "I'm so sorry, Hope." He told me he couldn't do it anymore and that he was indeed leaving. Those words hit me like a ton of bricks and at dinner I sat and felt my insides shatter. Mom and I didn't even end up eating, she drove us to the beach. We walked out and sat in the middle of the sand. It was dark and it was still. And I sobbed. But my mom never said, "I told you so." She never put my face in the ground, she sympathized with me so deeply in this season.

We sat in silence for a good bit but she told me something that sank deeply. She said, "You need someone who can love you with a godly love" and though I didn't carry a belief at the time, I'll never forget that. I felt as if this meant I wasn't enough for him to stay. I felt forgotten. I felt betrayed. I felt like our feelings were one-sided. I felt like the one thing that I had I truly did lose. I felt worthless. And most of all, I felt like an idiot because my parents knew this is what was going to happen. Life kept unfolding and when he got back home, my only friend I had and him ended up getting together. And I never imagined that years later they would end up having a child together, too. So there I was in Florida, trying to start new after the only two people I trusted pierced my heart with the same knife.

We always hear the question, "If you had one piece of advice to give someone what would it be?" Mine is plain and simple. Use your ache. Day by day I am obtaining the deeper understanding that everything I know to do right is from everything I have done dreadfully wrong. And in the same way, everything that I know to be true, is from everything that I have seen to be absolutely corrupt. As my human hands turn through the brittle pages of life, my soul has caught on to the hidden fact that somewhere in the piles of heartache and loads of uncertainty - there has been a holy depiction of God's grace and faithfulness.

My soul has known ache as it's own family and they use to sit down together for their daily pity party. You see, my soul use to look at ache as if it was destructive and my heart perceived it to be fatal. But as the piles grew larger something whispered that there was a big piece my eyes kept overlooking. It took years of becoming alliances with despair when I realized that my ache was actually my greatest gift in the world. Why? Because there is a difference between seeing a blessing from God and seeing the heart of God in a blessing. And I learned that this entire time, my ache was the blessing. No longer did my soul look at ache as a fatality, but it had me opening up my hands as something special I would hold onto for the rest of my life.

Something that would benefit somebody else for the rest of their life. Something that had purpose, and something that was going to shape me into who I was suppose to be.

HONEST TRUTH

"The Lord is my shepherd; I shall not want.

He makes me lie down in green pastures.

He leads me beside still waters.

He restores my soul.

He leads me in paths of righteousness

for his name's sake.

Even though I walk through the valley of the shadow of death,

I will fear no evil,

for you are with me;

your rod and your staff,

they comfort me.

You prepare a table before me

in the presence of my enemies;

you anoint my head with oil;

my cup overflows.

Surely goodness and mercy shall follow me

all the days of my life,

and I shall dwell in the house of the Lord

forever."

Psalm 23:1-6 (ESV)

CHALLENGE

And there we are. In an aching gaze with our own nostalgia of spring in our lives. Back when the sun was there to bloom everything new and when our hearts felt what was paralyzed begin to move. But what we forget is that Spring cannot be alive without Winter and Winter cannot happen without Autumn. What we forget is that Winter holds the footing for the upcoming season and while we are hopelessly in love with Spring — we forget that Winter is in the process of removing what needs to be removed for Spring to blossom. And for that very reason, I taught myself to be expectantly in love with Winter.

Look around your life and ask yourself if your Winter season is trying to remove some things. Instead of fighting it, take a step back and consider the fact that there may be a few things that cannot be brought into the next season of your life. Instead of fighting it, ask the Lord to shift your perspective. And watch as your resistance turns into rejoicing.

REFLECTION

I. What does the phrase, "You have so much potential" mean to you? Is there anyone in your life you need to pull out the current strengths instead of pointing out their future potential?

II. Look back at your life from five years ago. Did you ever expect to make it through the things you were going through? How does that make you view what you may be going through now?

III. Was there ever a point in your life where you developed the belief that there was no belief? How did that help shape your belief you carry now?

IV. What ache has turned out to be your greatest blessing? What current ache are you experiencing that can turn out to be your greatest blessing?

CHAPTER 6

NO MEANS NO

Sixteen. With not a clue of who I was and clinically depressed with pills I kept abusing. I started leaning on cocaine at sixteen because marijuana just wasn't cutting it. I weighed 114 pounds and I was a longing search to try and fill a void where on some days, I would be in multiple beds that were not my own. If you've known brokenness.. I have, too. I dropped out of school at sixteen, because I had no hope. I would argue that a lot of devastating events in our lives are caused by our own actions and our decisions. But there are some things that take place out of our control that should never happen, regardless of who you are or where you're at.

There are some things that shouldn't be kept silent even when they world is shouting over you. Because real life happens, and I believe the world needs to wake up to it. And I hope I can serve as the one of the first, of many, voices to speak up.

UNSPOKEN REALITY: I KNOW I AM NOT THE ONLY ONE

In my sixteen year old body I clung onto alcohol and pills. Self harm was my friend, and smoking was my relief. And boys were my acceptance. I was fairly new at a school in Florida, but quickly I found the friend group of partiers. I didn't go to school much, because most days I couldn't get my body out of bed. But you never missed me at a party. Spring break came around, which meant I was getting out of bed everyday for a gathering. Because it's spring break, and that's what the world tells young people to do. I was home laying on my depression in bed as usual when I was invited to this huge party Tuesday night. These boys I was friends with at school were going to pick me up and I was going to hang out with the group and some others at the pre-game party.

I needed something to get my mind clear so I got up and let them come pick me up. It was a fun day, really. We were all friends just goofing off throughout the day, and when we arrived to the party that night I met up with my girl friends from school who were there. I call all of these people my friends, but they were not my friends. They were my gateways to alcohol and drugs, therefore I called them my friends. But they did not know anything about me or what all I was going through inwardly. That's not a friend and I believe that we throw around the term way too freely. If your group of people are encouraging you to get wasted to blur out problems, they are not your friends. If your group of people don't care to listen to what's really going on in your heart, they are not your friends.

If your group of people aren't pushing you towards your dream and holding you to a higher standard, they are not your friends. A friend pushes you to healthily deal your problems, not drink them down. A friend calls out your strengths and does what they can to see you use them. A friend doesn't let you blend in with what every one else participating in. This is an honest scene I'm laying out for whoever is reading, because these things are real. These things do happen. These things needs to be talked about. And these things do matter.

The people I was at this party with were all there to party, which we did. I don't remember much of that night. I had way too much to drink and with a combination of everything else I had taken, I couldn't hardly walk. I remember two of the boys walking me to the car and I remember them driving. I don't know who all was in the car, but I was already sick. The plan was for me to stay at my friend Cristina's house, she was really my friend. A good one too that always stuck by my side. Honest and kind. She's one of the few I can say that about still to this day. Unfortunately, like many girls have experienced, I never made it to her house that night. I don't remember much at all, but the few flashbacks I have, I remember well.

I remember laying on this ratty old bed. There were three boys in the room. And just my sixteen year old body. I couldn't move, I was so frail. I weighed maybe 115 pounds. I was physically ill, and I was entirely broken. One of the boys were by my face attempting to force oral sex, and I re-member quietly pushing out the word, "No", as the tears ran down my face. Because I didn't want that. The other boy was on top forcefully having sex with me, and I remember quietly pushing out the word, "No", as the tears ran down my face. Because I didn't want that. I was too gone to try and defend myself. I felt paralyzed with their hands on my wrists and arm on my neck. I remember frantically screaming in my head that they would stop. But all I could do was weakly say, "No."

I remember them taking turns while my vision went in and out. I blacked out drunk, and in some way I'm thankful that I wasn't fully awake in the duration of it. For a long time, I classified that night of being taken advantage of. But that is not the case. These high school boys committed rape. Brutally. I remember waking up the next morning and looking over to see the boys. Trying to process of what happened I remember stumbling my way down the hall of this old house to the bathroom. There were roaches on the wall and an awful stench in the air. I looked in the mirror and my hair was in a mess. Makeup smeared down my face. Bloodshot eyes. Underwear on backwards. That was my breaking point. And I remember looking in the mirror at my little sixteen year old face with fear in those pink eyes, hands trembling as I went to touch the tear stains on my cheeks and saying out loud,

"Why me?"

"How did I let this happen to myself?"

"Why?"

My phone was dead and I didn't know where I was because I was still fairly new to the area. One of the boys left and the other one was going to the gym. I got in the car with him in silence. Staring straight ahead I was still processing all that happened and I felt so sick. I couldn't find any words that seemed fitting to speak. So I remained silent. My friend Kyle came and picked me up from the gym to take to Cristina's. Kyle was like a brother to me, I leaned on him for a lot of things in this season of my life. When he picked me up you could see on his face that he knew what happened. But he comforted me and didn't try to save the day. And I appreciated that about him.

After I made it home later that evening, that same day the boys came back to my house. They were at my front door and again, as many of us have heard the same empty words, "I'm sorry". It was a petty apology with demands that I wouldn't say a word about it. I was so sick I didn't even take notice to their words and ended up in the hospital shortly after for alcohol poisoning and other wounds from what had taken place the night before. I didn't tell the nurse what happened, or my parents. I was severely dehydrated so I let that be the cause, and that was it. I spent the remainder of Spring Break glued to my depression in my bed. Reliving in my mind what happened and trying to make sense of it.

———————

In today's world, we hear stories of these things happening more and more often. Almost as if it has become something common. Which is really sickening if you think about it. I'm not here to fight for justice or to try and go back to expose those boys. I'm here to shed light on a very serious, and very common thing that has probably happened to more than one person you know and have a conversation with. We really don't know what people have encountered or gone through. It is so important for us to sit down with people and have soft eyes and open hearts. At the end of the week it was time to go back to school and it was a normal school day to me. But it wasn't like the others. There was this new app being popularly downloaded and used. It was this app where it was a screen and in a specific mile radius people could write posts anonymously, and people could like posts anonymously.

It was High School, obviously this app was only used to tear people apart. I hadn't downloaded it yet and the bell was about to ring for Spanish Class to start. This boy in my class came up to me laughing asking if I liked getting houdinied. Confusion swallowed my face and I couldn't answer him. When class started I slid my phone out of my pocket to quickly look up the definition and it meant, "When a girl/guy you just fooled around with decides to up and vanish without a trace leaving you simultaneously confused." I felt my insides begin to heat up and my heart beating heavy. I could feel my breathing become short and my eyes flooded with tears. My hands began to tremble and I picked up my stuff and literally ran out of class with anxiety following behind me. I sat in the bathroom stall vomiting and sobbing. I didn't have anyone that I wanted to turn to.

I didn't understand. Something like this only happened in movies, not in real life. Not to me. This was the first emotion I had felt in a long time and I couldn't shake it. I missed two classes after that and was walking into the cafeteria to find a seat. One of the boys from that night walked by me and sticking his nose in the air like he had never seen me before in his life. My heart sunk and it was that moment that I really didn't want to live anymore. I had thought about it before many times, but this time I desperately wanted to put action to my thoughts. I didn't want to live. Not carrying this with me. I thought that my life was heavy before all of this, and I was barely making it through with just that. But this was my tipping point.

I was strongly advised to download the app to see what was being said on it, so I did. And boy, I wish I didn't. Kids are so cruel. There were so many things written about the rape. Degrading, awful things. "Someone needs to get hope a spot on a show 'Sex Brought Me to the Emergency Room'," "She's claiming rape for attention when really she wanted it." I hadn't spoke of it to anybody and was beginning to have an anxiety attacks regularly every hour. I felt as if every room I walked into people were looking at me and pointing fingers. I had no one to talk to. My best friend that I had from Georgia was sleeping with the boy who I built life on, my GPA was under a 1.0, I had to wear long sleeves everyday in the blazing Summer heat because self harm was very real and I spent more time in the bathrooms throwing up from anxiety than I did sitting stable. I was at my end and there was no sense of light in the future for me.

If this is how hateful the world was, then I didn't want to be in it anymore.

HIGH SCHOOL DROP OUT

So, I threw in the towel and dropped out. At sixteen in the tenth grade. I was a pill head, and after I dropped out I was in desperation for some kind of way out. The only thoughts that ran through my head for weeks were plans to end the life I carried. My "goodbye" letter was written over and over. It's by the grace of God himself I sit here today, writing to you. For someone who is named Hope, there was not an ounce of hope in those eyes. I did not physically die. As much as I wanted to, I didn't. But my soul was lifeless. And in some ways, a dead soul is heavier than a dead body.

That's why my heart is so sensitive to the youth. So sensitive to people. I haven't experienced everything in life by no means, but I have experienced the feelings of not wanting to feel again. If you're reading this, I sincerely do love you. As weird as that sounds, I really do.

To the One Who May Be Contemplating Their Life:

Hey.
You still matter.

I love you. My sweet friend, you are more. And there is more. You matter. I would never dare to tell you that what you're feeling is diminutive. That what you're feeling is of no worth. I would never dare to tell you that I understand your heart and your life even the least bit. And I would never dare to tell you that you are capable to get through it. Though I know you are, I believe there is a time for tough love and there is a time to press pause and sit down with understanding eyes. I don't know what has been written in your story, I do not have the power to grasp that. I cannot tell you that your situation is going to get better. I cannot tell you that people will treat you kindly or that you will receive apologies your soul is aching for. You are not alone. I promise you this. You are not alone. You are not alone. You are not alone. My friend, there is someone who needs you. And I know what you're thinking. "Why would I want to be there for someone if no one has ever been there for me?" Because. What if someone was there for you? What if someone noticed you in your pain? What if you crossed paths with someone and it changed the whole course of your life? I don't know the pain you are feeling, but I can tell you that your pain will be your greatest asset of your life if you let it. If you let it, your pain will draw out your most inner being and will shape you into the person you've always wanted to be that you didn't even know.

It's not over for you. I wanted it to be over for me. Oh my gosh, I wanted it to be over for me. But can I tell you that sitting here as I write this in the brisk cold of February, I have never been more humbled that I have my pain to look back on. And I'm believing that you too, will come to that place. I can't help but smirk as I write this. But if you have dealt with this, don't you know that there is something so big coming for you right around the corner? I'm about to flip this table over and start shouting in joy for you.

The one's that get so close to the point of almost ending their life are the one's you have the most to offer to the world. That's not an actual fact, but that sits deep in my belief. Life got so brutally cruel that it almost took the most precious thing you hold. You cannot tell me that doesn't mean something big. You have something to offer to people in an incredibly raw and inherent way. When you get through this, you literally have a life ring in the palm of your hand for somebody else. You my friend, will now carry something that the world is in desperation to have a touch of. You now have a deep rooted strength about you that can never be uprooted.

You now have a hope in your soul that will not be touched. You now have words to speak that hold a heavy meaning because you lived it. And you overcame it. This, this is something to throw a party for. And I didn't see it that way for a long time, I didn't choose a lot of things that are written in my story and that's the thing I learned. I do not want to rewrite it. That's why I'm writing it you in hopes that my mess will inspire you to embrace your mess. Because we are all messy people trying to cover it up. But I don't want to cover it. I want to embrace it with you.

I love you.

I so believe in you.

And I want to celebrate you for the rest of our days.

Love,

The Broken Sixteen Year Old Girl Who Made It

SOMEONE ELSE SAYING YES TO JESUS

In the midst of my mess, I found myself at church one Sunday night for youth service. I don't know why I was there, but I thank God for it to this day. In my short shorts and crop top, I went. And that night was a night that got me to where I am today. This girl approached me and started talking to me. Her name was Stephanie and she didn't know much about my life at all. She was asking about me and actually seemed like she had interest. I told her how I just dropped out, and she began to tell me how I need to apply to this college program that she's in. In my head, I was like, "Did you not just listen to the fact that I'm sixteen?" (I was rude back in my heathen days).

She told me how really all it was a big group of people who hung out all the time and building relationships. In my mind, I was like okay I have nothing in my life right now. So I applied. And with orientation in the next few days, they went against all their rules and guidelines and accepted me in. This was the first place that accepted me as I was. I didn't have to be something that I was not, or put on a front. I was me, and that was enough.

It's funny because life has a way of pulling out the very worst in us so that God can create the very best out of us. And in those times it can be so effortless to throw up our hands and call a quits. It can be so fitting to shrink back and go an alternative route. But over the years I've been thinking and with wide eyes I realized that the only reason I was able to know God is because somebody before me was obedient to God. If the person who first introduced me to the Lord had ever decided to put a wall up when things got hard or chose to go down their own path when things were unclear — I stand confident that there is a big chance I may have not met them at the time that I did. But because they chose to keep their feet planted and because they chose to let God use their ache, I was able to know God.

Because you are choosing to hold the hand of God in whatever your season may look like right now, someone else is going to be able to know Him. Because of you. And I don't know about you but I am so thankful for the person who chose to keep pushing through. Let's be that person who keeps pushing through. Because somebody is going to need you. And what a holy privilege that is.

I walked up to this orientation and I very quickly realize that this was not a real college. This was a hard core ministry bootcamp kind of deal. I sat there as they read off all of the rules, such as curfew being 10PM, no texting the opposite sex, workouts every morning at 7AM, all kinds of bizarre stuff. I sat there and cried because I did not know what I got myself into. I remember leaving orientation bitter as can be, because there no way getting out of it now.

That night I was looking over all the rules and went out to a party and broke many, many of those rules where I showed up to our beach orientation the next morning hungover. To this day, I am not in my first year class's group picture because I was by the bathrooms throwing up while they took it. (Poor decisions with Hope part...?) I wouldn't say that this school was for everyone. It was very intense but for where I was at in my life I needed that. Was the school perfect? Absolutely not. But they were the gateway who introduced my heart to the Lord. Therefore, I am grateful. As I said, this school was not really a school. The first day of school we had workouts, which was humorous because I hadn't worked out since I was twelve and was in ballet.

I walk up to the basketball court and when it hit 7AM they told us we were running three miles. I stood there and stared at them because I was not running that. I didn't run. I didn't workout. I didn't sweat. I didn't do the outdoors. And they were telling me we were about to run three miles with all these people I didn't know? Interesting. But hey, I ended up pushing my way through and here we are. Through running laps, through pulling weeds, sleeping on an island with tin foil that students had to kayak to for hours, through eating cow tongue and being tied up in the cold for six hours, through laying on the ground pretending I was slain in the spirit so no one would talk to me, and through the chaos of it all, I found the Lord that year. I may write another book just about this school. But, yes. That was me. I dropped out at sixteen then started ministry at sixteen.

This school had crazy events we had to do and that's where all that came from. But through it all I realized that it would have taken more faith to not believe anything than to ignore everything of who He is. We were in Tennessee on a Cabin Retreat and we were having a worship night. I felt my eyes tear up and I was fighting so hard whatever this feeling was. And I can't sit here and try to explain my experience with Jesus in this book. But I can tell you that in the softest yet most intense way, I felt myself broke. In a holy way. It was a radical change. A radical rescue. And the safest new home I ever knew. He changed everything.

Throughout the years I think we have all asked the question, "Will I alter my circumstances or will my circumstances alter me?" I think we have all stepped over traces of God because uncertainty held our eyes. We have made decisions that we knew were adamant and choosing to follow through with them was like reading a book with the last chapter glued shut. We don't get to choose how life unfolds in our lap and we are not gifted with the understanding of why things happen and even more so, why they didn't happen. But I do think sometimes we have to sort through the cluttered shelves of our heart.

I do think we have to realize we can only fit so many words into a sentence before we forget that words are sometimes used for things other than filling emptiness. I think what we are quick to forget is that the last chapter of the book will unfold when the time is right. And that is not a time we decide. So until then my friend, it's our own job to keep graciously moving through all the chapters leading up to that end piece. And I learned that it is not a bad place for us to be at. In fact, it's the place where we should be welcoming with open hands.

Because in a holy turn around, it's the greatest refining gift we can hold. *If we let it.*

HONEST TRUTH

"I'll never forget the trouble, the utter lostness,
the taste of ashes, the poison I've swallowed.
I remember it all—oh, how well I remember—
the feeling of hitting the bottom.
But there's one other thing I remember,
and remembering, I keep a grip on hope:
God's loyal love couldn't have run out,
his merciful love couldn't have dried up.
They're created new every morning.
How great your faithfulness!
I'm sticking with God (I say it over and over).
He's all I've got left.
God proves to be good to the man who passionately waits,
to the woman who diligently seeks.
It's a good thing to quietly hope,
quietly hope for help from God.
It's a good thing when you're young
to stick it out through the hard times.
When life is heavy and hard to take,
go off by yourself. Enter the silence.
Bow in prayer. Don't ask questions:
Wait for hope to appear.
Don't run from trouble. Take it full-face.
The "worst" is never the worst.
Why? Because the Master won't ever
walk out and fail to return.
If he works severely, he also works tenderly.
His stockpiles of loyal love are immense.
He takes no pleasure in making life hard,
in throwing roadblocks in the way:"

Lamentations 3:19-33 (ESV)

CHALLENGE

Memory lane is generally where people step on their gas pedal as hard as they can to speed on and pass it by in hopes of not having to remember anything. But I think it's good to take a glance back in the rearview mirror. In the small victories, to recall that God is God and He is constant. And in the devastating pits, to peep a glimpse of where you are now. That yeah, perhaps life once felt like a nightmare you never would wake from and the future was just a big ole blur. But look at you now now — alive, breathing, and reading this. You must be doing something right and there MUST be something bigger ahead. I look back at where life seemed as if it was my adversary and when everything that mattered kept slipping through my fingers. Where I did not see a way out of the ditch I did not even dig myself into. But I see now, that were was something ahead. And it was something so necessary. So necessarily good. And you know what? It's something good for you too, my friend. Keep going. KEEP pushing. Take a look back and see where God has brought you from. Dig deep and see what felt as if the end of the world actually had good at the bottom of it.

REFLECTION

I.   What does the "To the one who may be contemplating life" letter speak to you?

II. Who was the someone else who said yes to Jesus that introduced you?

III. What in your life has pulled out the very worst in you that allowed God to create the very best out of you? How different would your life be if the very worst never happened?

IV. What has happened in your life or what is currently happening in your life that you ought to be welcoming with open hands rather than sprinting the other way? What do you think you need to allow God to create a refining gift out of? What do you think stops you from allowing him to do so?

The Second Table

CHAPTER 7

COMPROMISE IS FOR THE ALTAR

Leadership first and foremost is laying compromise at the altar. The word compromise means to accept standards lower than desired and to become vulnerable and function less effectively. In one of my own greatest moments of compromising, I had written this blog.

"The wall beside the bed in my room is a light grey. A pleasant color might I say. On it, is five holes from where I had previously nailed pictures. On it, there are three scratches that I can see. And on it, there's a good bit of scuff marks at the bottom. Although, the more I sit here and stare, another default that I didn't see the first time appears. As pleasant as the wall may seem, the longer I examine it, the more the rough edges I see. This wall and I share a lot in common. At a glance, you could look at me and think congenially. However, if you take time to examine me, you will quickly find that I have some holes in my life, a few scratches, and a good bit of scuff marks. And as congenial I may seem, the longer you examine, the rougher edges you'll see. I'm in my second year of ministry school, I have two parents who are still together that love and support me, I have strong friendships that care for me, I have a bright future ahead of me, while having more than I need provided for me.

How can one be so despondent and lost, they say? What I don't understand is that I turned from everything towards Jesus, passionately pursuing Him. And yet I find myself today, feeling as if I never turned towards Him, in a concentrated stare at the wall. How can one be so despondent and lost, they say? It's scary to have been in such a pursuit of Jesus and then to look at yourself and not even be recognizable. The longer I sit and evaluate each piece of my life, the more unsatisfied I am. How does one get to this point? Could it be that my foundation in Christ was not yet established the way I had thought? Maybe I was in the wrong place at the wrong time? Or is it possible there was different path I was suppose to be taking than ministry? Or the big question that has been in the back of my head; is God even real and I have just been foolish and blinded to it all? If you've ever been in this place I am currently in, I have such compassion for you.

Because there's almost no words for it. It's like you know what you once had with God, but now you feel as if there's nothing. It's like you thought you were good and on the right path, but now everything is debatable and questionable. Yet, through it all, the concept that I can't comprehend is that in my heart, I know that God is good. Even when everything else tells me different. No, I don't have the perfect ending to this post of my thoughts. But, deep in my heart I know God is surely faithful. And I know He will lift whoever, including myself, out of the place that they're in. Why? Because He is God. And He always has been, and He always will be. Even when the image of Him is faint, or even more, when you feel you've turned the opposite way. He is still God. And in my heart, I know that He is good."

In the midst of all my mess, the Lord was still near to my heart. And still spoke so clearly to me. I blew my second year of ministry school, like I almost got kicked out. Of ministry school. I guess it was a pattern in my life? Getting kicked out of youth group then almost kicked out of ministry school. After knowing God this happened. All because I didn't keep my eyes on Him. One decision can quite literally change the whole direction of your life in an instant. And I learned that the hard way. But the hard way doesn't intimidate God. He'll still use it.

DADDY-DAUGHTER DATES

Growing up, I watched my dad selflessly serve my mom and bring her home roses once a week. I don't think there was ever a week where he didn't, and occasionally he would bring me home a rose, too. It wasn't thought of too much at the moment, but looking back and seeing now, all of these "so called men" not even having the thought cross their mind to buy their girlfriend roses, I look back and I appreciate it. My dad taught me what a gentleman looked like before I had the option to allow society to teach me what one looked like, and I admired that. I sat in the passenger seat more times than I count while he took me on daddy-daughter dates to dinner and bowling. Sometimes hiking. But my favorite, oh my favorite was the daddy daughter dances.

Mom would spend hours, and I mean hours doing my hair and makeup. Finding me a dress to look like I was about to walk the runway, and shoes that would catch the eye of whoever would walk by. All leading up to a fancy dinner at a nice restaurant an eight year old had no business eating at. I remember asking the server if they had chicken fingers on the menu, and each time the answer was no. I don't remember what I would end up eating, but it was never chicken fingers of macaroni. As I said earlier, it wasn't thought of too much at the moment, but looking back and seeing now men in relationships not have the decency to even take their girlfriend to dinner, I look back and appreciate it.

As the night went on we would arrive to the dance. He would park the car and would jump out and run to the other side of the car to open my door before I could. Extending his hand to help me out and hold out my coat for me to put on. We would walk up to the dance and he would already be pulling the door open for me and signaling for me to walk in first. It wasn't thought of too much at the moment, but looking back and seeing now girls open their own door, and following their boyfriend into places, I look back and appreciate it. I listened to his seemingly never ending prayers every night before I went to sleep. If I can be honest, it was the most annoying thing. I couldn't hardly stand it. Some days when I really wasn't in the mood to have him pray over me, I would race up to my room after dinner and jump in bed and act like I was already sleeping. Or I would go to the bathroom to avoid him until I heard his bedroom door shut, and then I would come out. Petty, right?

I would peek out the window as I was a young girl to see him reading his Bible devotionals. Every. Single. Morning. My dad was the first one there to pick me up at two in the morning when I was somewhere I wasn't suppose to be, to being the first one there at my car accident scene to being the one I can solely rely on for anything, however absurd it may be. That's how a Father is suppose to be.

I've been through a lot in my life, but one thing I have not experienced was a poor Father figure. So hear me out for just a moment. I want to sincerely apologize to all of the ladies out there who didn't have the best Dad growing up, or who didn't even have one at all. I will not tell you that I understand what it's like. Because I simply don't, and I think that is one of the biggest misconceptions today. Proclaiming that we understand exactly what someone is feeling when we have not personally been through it ourselves. Even more so, often enough two people can be going through the exact same thing but handle it very differently. Everyone feels in their own way. Everyone deals with life in their own way. Therefor I will not tell you that I understand and I know how it feels. But what I will tell you is that I'm sorry. I am so very sorry, my girl. Because you are worth more than that and I'm so sorry you may have grown up not knowing that. If you are one of those ladies, I am so proud of you. Here you are, reading this. Breathing, and alive. Strong. Stable. Smart. Independent. Here you are, one heck of a woman and I am so proud of you.

You are capable to do anything, and you are not held to the mishaps or hardships you experienced. My girl, do not let anyone tell you differently. If you're a man reading this, be that godly man to your daughter. Whether that's now or later. I never would have been where I am today if it wasn't for my dad and I am always replaying our conversations in my head when the seasons get rough. He has been my rock, and I encourage you to be that, too. I learned a lot in my dates with Dad and I have held all of it dear to my heart. So in the same way, having Daddy-Daughter dates with God is something I learned to hold dear to my heart, too. I learn something every time I've set up a date with Him, and even when I don't, He still slides in some kind of learning lesson for me to see.

Although, I think the whole concept of seeking God is skewed. Having intimacy with God portrayed as sitting in the church pews with your Sunday best. Or having to raise your hands in every worship song to show that you're really saved. Or having to spend every breathing second with other Christians and serving in some capacity. It's whack. I love reading about God and all the crazy unfathomable things He's done, it makes me proud to call Him my own. I love worshipping, because it's like giving to God what He can't give himself. And I love serving, helping out others is what I believe we're called to do. But, I also love just sitting in stillness, the good kind. In the quiet, knowing He's right there.

Looking at the leaves turning yellow, and having a few fall down on my face and not even be mad about it. Watching the water stroll down the stream, exactly how it's suppose to. Because God has a way of creating things exactly as it ought to be. Looking at the beauty that isn't man made and having God say, "Yes, it's for you." without me even asking. For me, my favorite kind of seeking God is sitting in His thoughtfully put together por-traits and having my heart open to receive for when He speaks. That sounds way spiritual but I promise it's not. Just simply admiring whats around me wherever I go. And I think He's the same with us, just smiling down at our little lives admiring His work, but always being ready to listen when we want to talk to Him.

I had to learn that it was okay to not have a schedule sometimes, and I feel we all need to grasp hold of that little yet big truth. In fact, it's the unscheduled moments that have made the greatest impact on me. With God, and with my own dad. I remember one time when dad and I were just sitting on a bench outside, he told me that if the boy I'm going out with doesn't open the door for me, then to run. That if the boy I'm going out with doesn't love the Lord, then to run. I always thought he was crazy, you know, telling me how I was going to be the head and not the tail and how I was going to accomplish more than I can imagine.

But man, watching the way he lives his life inspires me. He is the true definition of a godly man who selflessly loves, and I am so thankful. He never compromised in anything he did. He was all in or he was all out. He never accepted standards lower than what was desired. Moving out really did take a toll on my heart when I would go months without seeing him, trying to figure out this life thing all grown up. It was rough. But sweet memories made my day everyday. I remember I said in the 5th grade that he was my hero, and shoot, he still is. Daddy-Daughter dates may sound cheesy. But it was on a day where I set aside time specifically to spend the day with just me and God that changed my life forever. I was doing ministry. I had it going for me but it was like I hit a wall and I couldn't go further. I would catch myself slipping back into old thought patterns here and there. I noticed that there was something still attached that needed change. And it was a compromised spirit that I had been carrying my entire life.

CHURCH CULTURE

Never have I ever been a believer of the whole, "You have to have everything together, and if you don't then at least make yourself look like you do." That is not genuine, and in a world full of humans we are desperate for authenticity. I'll tell you what's admirable, It's when someone just lays it all out on the table shaking their head because they're exhausted. That takes guts nowadays. Living in a perfect painted world with eyes watching every move you make anticipating for one wrong one, to make it known that you've taken a few messy steps because some days are just flat out messy. I think that's the biggest misconception, associating days with your entire life. But just because you have a messy day doesn't mean you have a messy life.

We just have to learn to brush it off and take another whack at it. If anything is admirable, it's owning our messiness and proudly trying again. That is strength. In a world that screams perfection, softly fighting back to show that perfection is unlikely. I think that's what Jesus is after. The one who doesn't scream perfection. As I mentioned before why church wasn't for me, I'm sure there are more people who can relate than we think.

"Church is fun, God is great. But church people? Lol."

Our first reaction to this response is probably, "Yikes." But I mean. Do we really disagree with it? One time I asked the question, "What keeps you from going to church?" on one of my social media platforms and I let anyone respond. I clarified that regardless if someone was a believer or not, I was very interested in hearing their response, because every answer matters.

Here's a few that people sent in:

"Going alone and walking in just for everyone to clique up and not feel welcomed."

"What keeps me there is Jesus... but in my own strength? I would leave because of serious hurt."

"The people there..."

"Depression that's overwhelming to other Christians"

"People only care about those inside the walls"

"Judgmental people inside of church"

"Walking in alone and feeling judged"

Ouch. I sat in a stare at just these few answers because they are so raw and honest. These answers were not made up and they were not answers that were sent as a jab towards any particular person or place. These answers were from real people who have encountered real experiences at real churches. I fear that we as Christians have compromised the Gospel for our own comfort at times. Inside the church world, the question is asked, "How do you successfully grow your ministry?" And honestly, I've been stuck on finding an answer to this for the past three years. Any organization that has a product in which they believe in has a goal to share it with the world and grow their company. Because they believe in what they're doing and they are confident that their product is the best out there.

Just as any organization, many churches operate the same way. They believe in what they're doing and who they're doing it for, therefore they want to expand their reach and grow their attendance. Because they are confident that their God is the only God. It's not meant to be a competition. Even though, unfortunately, some make it out to be. So, how do you successfully grow your ministry?

New lighting system? Sweet. That will make the social media feed look sick. But cool lights don't impact somebody's heart and soul. Free food at every event? Sweet. That will attract all the college kids because we're all balling on a budget (lol, Lord help us.) But free food doesn't impact somebody's heart and soul. First time guest gift bag? Sweet. That will be a neat thing that they won't expect. But a cookie cutter free gift doesn't impact somebody's heart and soul. More of a social media push on service weeks? Sweet. That will show we're all excited for the next service. But a picture on a screen doesn't impact somebody's heart and soul.

All of these things are so great. All of these things so helpful. All of these things will absolutely attract somebody for the first time. Maybe a second time. And if we're lucky, maybe even a third time. But let's be honest with ourselves — none of these things are sustainable to keep somebody around. What impacts somebody's heart and soul for the first time? A genuine, "Hi. What's your name?" And remembering their name. What impacts somebody's heart and soul for the first time? Sitting down with a set of clear eyes ready to listen to their story. What impacts somebody's heart and soul for the first time? Preparing a seat for them at your table before they can even ask. What impacts somebody's heart and soul for the first time? Getting their information and following up with them the next week. What impacts somebody's heart and soul for the first time? Simply caring about who they are as a person.

If we can get really real, we can be honest and admit that as Christians, we do a crappy job at representing Jesus sometimes. When I think of Jesus, I think of someone who is present in the moment. Who doesn't have his eyes locked on his phone refreshing his Instagram feed while in a room full of people who are lost. I think of someone who is kind. On his good day and his bad day. Because his character is what determines his response to people, not his current stressful situation. I think if Jesus were here today, He wouldn't be scouting out the area where the preachers and "big named" people are hanging out.

Am I saying I think Jesus would down at the club busting a few moves and sharing a few drinks? Not exactly lol. But I do, I really do believe He wouldn't dissipate every time a partier was near. I think He would sit back, and have a conversation. Because a conversation is always more productive than an assumption. I don't believe Jesus would drive down the crazy one way streets in Atlanta looking at all the homeless and labeling them as addicts because "It was their own decision". I think He would pull over time to time, buy a sandwich, and go and sit with them. Not shoving the Bible in their face but just being there with a set of clear eyes.

I can't picture Jesus pushing his way to the front trying to show off in front of his leaders. But I see him slipping out from the crowd and sitting at the table with the person who was all alone. I don't believe that when a new face showed up on a Sunday morning at church with the stench of alcohol that Jesus would be turning around raising his eye brow to make 'that' eye contact with his peers. You know, the look you give each other without having to say a word because you're both thinking the same thing. No... not at all. I believe the BIGGEST grin would appear on His face, that you would see Heaven in His eyes as they locked with theirs, and He would walk up to them with a hug so thrilled that they were there.

Making them feel right at home, like you and I ought to do better. Because celebrating and smiling in the middle of ache and judgement is exactly what it means to be a follower of Jesus. And in today's culture, everyone is going to be looking at you saying "What is wrong with them?" But they are seeing something in you that is more than what they have seen in humanity, and if you keep being the whacko who just keeps loving and celebrating everybody and anybody — eventually the people who were questioning will be so curious that they'll want to join you.

So… the question is asked, "How do you successfully grow your ministry?" And I found that the answer is actually quite simple. Care about people. Especially the one's that no one else seems to. When people know you love them, and people know you care about them — you will never have to ask them to stay. When people know you love them, and people know you care about them — they'll be the one's who are telling their friends how different we are and how they have to come.

And here's the funny thing. Loving and caring are most effective when words are not present.

Let's smile a little more.
Let's open our circle a little more.
Let's be like Jesus, a little bit more
Let's lay down compromise, a whole lot more.

HONEST TRUTH

"Summing up: Be agreeable, be sympathetic, be loving, be compassionate, be humble. That goes for all of you, no exceptions. No retaliation. No sharp-tongued sarcasm. Instead, bless—that's your job, to bless. You'll be a blessing and also get a blessing.

Whoever wants to embrace life
   and see the day fill up with good,
Here's what you do:
   Say nothing evil or hurtful;
Snub evil and cultivate good;
   run after peace for all you're worth.
God looks on all this with approval,
   listening and responding well to what he's asked;
But he turns his back
   on those who do evil things."

   1 Peter 3:8-12 (MSG)

CHALLENGE

If all you've ever known is failure, that's great. That's all I knew, too. But I was able to learn to know a God who only knew success and He taught me all about it. Especially in the times where I literally tripped over my own feet trying to run away, He was there painting a picture of what was ahead. And it got me every time. He's doing that for you, too. You CAN do this. You ARE loved. Whatever season you're in, He's still the SAME God. The most mournful harm we could do to ourselves is to refuse to look at our hearts honestly for who we are and live it out. The world can be screaming in your face for being rare, but the piercing shriek is only a cover up for desperation to do the same. I promise, it makes a difference when you're you. And it makes a difference when you're you on purpose.

Communicate who you really are through everything you do, and give the world your best show. Even if it's messy sometimes. We'll watch and cheer you on. Find something you thoroughly enjoy doing this week, and own it.

REFLECTION:

I. It's scary to have been in such a pursuit of Jesus and then to look at yourself and not even be recognizable. Have you experienced this? What led to you to that point? How did you get out of it?

II. What does seeking God mean to you?

III. What does compromise mean to you?

IV. When you think of church culture, what do you think of? Do you think church people are a big reason why people don't enjoy church? How can you and I make a difference in this?

V. When you think of Jesus as someone walking the halls of a church, what do you think he would be doing? Who do you think he would be talking to?

CHAPTER 8
FAITH AS A VALUE

*"**W**hen he came down from the mountain, great crowds followed him. **2** And behold, a leper came to him and knelt before him, saying, "Lord, if you will, you can make me clean." **3** And Jesus stretched out his hand and touched him, saying, "I will; be clean." And immediately his leprosy was cleansed."*
Matthew 8:1-3 (ESV)

The Leper was a man in bondage to something he couldn't get rid of on his own. But who was bold enough to go to Jesus for a healing touch in front of a crowd who disowned him. *The Leper didn't compromise his faith.* Compromise will always make the conquerer into the one being conquered.

ENOUGH IS ENOUGH

I think we all inadvertently accept less than what we stand for sometimes. Maybe because we get frustrated, or maybe because we think what we stand for is too much at times. Throughout my years I have noticed that on the really demanding days where everything is upside down – I found it really manageable to just take the short end of the stick and call it a day. To say "It's easier to remain in this than to put in the effort to change this."

It's not easy but we need to learn how to get tired of tolerating conditions that are not in line with our surety. It's not popular, but we need to learn how to get tired of saying yes to things that our hearts are shouting no. It's not effortless, but we need to learn how to get tired of trying on peoples opinions as if those are what we are going to wear when everything is all said and done. You see, settling is more than just accepting less than. Settling is choosing comfort over calling. And I have never known someone worth looking up to because of their comfortability and commitment to average. But it's the people who learned how to get tired of certain habits, certain friendships, certain relationships (come on somebody), and certain ways of thinking — those people. The people who are silently different simply because of their character. Let's be one of those people. for ourselves, and for the people who may look up to us one day, too.

The thing about the Leper is he was walking around with something he was cursed with that was out of his control. There was not a single thing he could have done on his own to get rid of his condition. Like many of us, there are things that were passed down to us that we couldn't stop. There were things that have happened to us that we couldn't stop. There are habits that we carry that we cannot get rid of. There are mindsets that consume us that we can't change. Back in the day, as long as someone had a disease they were unclean. They had to live alone and away from everybody.

But here's the thing about Jesus. There are legalistic people who have complained that Jesus violated the law in this story. For it was completely unlawful to touch a leper. If anyone touched a leper they were forever ceremonially unclean. And there goes Jesus. Doing His thing. Leprosy begins with the loss of all sensation in some part of the body. The muscles waste away, so you because numb to feeling what is wrong. The tendons contract until the hands are like claws. There spreads to the hands and feet. Then comes the progressive loss of fingers and toes, until in the end an entire hand or a whole foot may drop off. It is a terrible progressive and slow death in which a person dies inch by inch.

So this man, the Leper, had a condition that he could no longer feel because it progressed so rapidly. He had a condition that was essentially killing him day by day, and there was no human touch that could relieve him of this tragedy. But what I admire is the Leper came to Jesus by himself despite how many discouragements he would encounter.

He knew how terrible his problem was.

He knew that other people gave up on him as having a hopeless condition.

He had no promise that Jesus would heal him.

He must have felt ashamed and alone in the crowd.

"Lord, if You are willing"

The leper had no doubt whatsoever about the ability of Jesus to heal. He was bold. His only question was if Jesus was willing to heal. The Leper was not suppose to come into human contact but by his actions of silently saying, enough is enough — he was reconstructing human faith.

When I was eighteen in my second year of my first ministry school in Florida, after following Jesus whole-heartedly I willingly let go of the hand of Jesus and fell back into all my old ways. I was focusing under our Connection's Pastor, working my way into a job position, and leading High School girls at youth. In a matter of one night, I lost absolutely everything. From being on the very top, to face planting at the very bottom. I had still been entertaining things that I let go of when I met Jesus, and sin crept in through the crack I left open and it destroyed me. I was back to lying, doing drugs, sleeping around, and everything under the moon. After knowing Jesus and almost landing a job in ministry.

There is something different about falling back into things you believed you were delivered from. It does something to your soul and makes you contemplate if you ever really even knew Jesus. Coming out of that life-style for the first time is tough. But falling back in and trying to come out for a second time, seems impossible. My school didn't kick me out. They kept me and tried to walk with me though what was happening. But in my own ignorance and stubbornness, I wanted to be left alone. It was in this time of me sprinting away from God and drowning myself in self-escapes that the Lord stopped me in my tracks to open my eyes to what was being planted back in Gainesville, Georgia. The church that my parents originally moved us to was starting a ministry school and I will never forget seeing a post about it and hearing the Lord tell me to go.

While I was caught up in my sin. While I was ignoring every sign from Him he throwing my way. While I was living for myself and leaning towards my old belief that there was no belief. In the middle of my mess the Lord spoke the loudest. And my first reaction was, absolutely not.

WHAT IS WAS WILL NOT ALWAYS BE

In a world full of the mentality of 'What's next and who's next' — I feel my human bones inside my skin begin to soften at the thought that there is a God who can count the beat of my heart from a million miles a way. A God who has this zeal of awakening our hearts to the quiet truth that we are so known even in a crowd that is so obscure. And my bones are softened to know that in a noisy room of comparison and expectation, He could pick me up out from the crowd just from hearing my sigh.

What an honor it is to be known and what an honor it is to be taught how to know. You see, we need to train our silence to speak up. And train our bluntness to sit softly. Let's train our heart to trust more unhurried, because even with the best intentions, a heart is deserving for us to be careful. Let's train our eyes to flip through the pages of the room we are in. Because we need to not be so interested with what people think of us. But rather be dedicated to how people feel around us. And for this very reason, let's cherish the ability to have our own mess and our own quirks. All for the purpose of sitting down in the crowd with another human heart and giving their lips the freedom to say, 'Me too'.

What an honor it is to be known by Him.
And what an honor it is to be taught how to know like Him.

I don't believe the Leper was the least bit interested in what people thought of him. I genuinely believe deep down, his heart was dedicated to how people felt around him. I believe he wanted to be the person he was made to be. I believe he had a dream, and he had a vision of what he wanted his life to look like. I believe he hit a point of realization that he couldn't do it on his own. And I believe that was the point Jesus was waiting for Him to hit so he could fall into grace. So Jesus could so kindly whisper to him, "Because of your faith, what it was will not always be."

I had never been so certain that the Lord was in something when he put it on my heart to move back to Georgia. Which is so ironic, because if anything didn't make sense — it was moving back to Gainesville, the home of heartache and bad decisions. Even more-so, moving back to the church where I was kicked out of youth group from. Yep. When I was fifteen I was literally removed from youth group and I despised the church so much that my mom would pay me $100 a Sunday to sit in main service with her. Then I would use that money to maintain my bad habits.

In this season I felt as if I was blind dog just following after my masters voice with not a clue of where I was going or what I was doing. All I knew is that I had to go and that was all there was to it. No one was on board with me going back to Gainesville, because of everything that had previously happened when I was fifteen. And when I fell back into my old ways during my second year of ministry school, that happened when I was in Gainesville, too. So to pack up all my things and move back to the place where my sin lived while I was still living in sin made no sense what-so-ever. But, I knew what the Lord said and something in my soul couldn't shake it.

Nothing beneficial ever happened in Georgia and even in my own head I was confused and thought for sure something was not right. But I have learned to let the Lord do what He wants and for my mouth to hush up and just go. It wasn't until a week after I moved and was settled in my apartment that I had my enough is enough moment. Orientation for the new ministry school was in three days and I had just come out of a week full of parties and wild living. I remember sitting in my room in a deep stare at my wall.

I knew how terrible my problem was.

I knew there was not anything I could do to stop repeating this cycle.

I knew that I did not have the power to break off the generational patterns in my life.

I'll never forget taking two sheets of paper. On the first sheet, I wrote out every characteristic of the person who I knew I wanted to be. On the second sheet, I wrote out every characteristic of the person who I was in that moment. And I compared the two side-by-side. I took it to Jesus and just like the Leper, "Lord, if you are willing." Because I had the realization I couldn't do it on my own. And that was the point Jesus was waiting for so he could kindly whisper, "Because of your faith, what it was will not always be."

Life change does not always happen in an alter inside of a church. Life change can happen when your heart sits down to rest and simply says, "Jesus, help me." And mine was in my bedroom.

HONEST TRUTH

"And after you have suffered a little while, the God of all grace, who has called you to his eternal glory in Christ, will himself restore, confirm, strengthen, and establish you."

1 Peter 5:10 (ESV)

CHALLENGE

This is slowly what I've learned... a mind that is unfocused is incredibly vulnerable to other opinions, our own selfishness, and our old patterns. All of which openly invite a downward tug on our thoughts and can lead us to an alternative route for our lives than what we really wanted. Everything starts in our mind and the neatest thing is that WE get to choose what we focus on. When our thinking processes become scattered we become more and more confused and after going a thousand different directions at once — we end up becoming directionless.

I don't know who needs to hear this but let's get back to the root of who He is. Let's refocus our mind and our heart on Him and who He is. Him who is not just this big God way up in the Heavens and all that. But Him who is our constant support. Our closest friend. And our biggest fan.

REFLECTION

I.   What does settling mean to you?

II. Has there been a time in your life where in your eyes it was easier to remain in your struggle than it was to put in the effort to change? How did you navigate through that struggle?

III. What in your life now do you need to say, "Enough is enough" to? What are practical action steps you can start now?

IV. What in your life do you need to say, "Lord, if you are willing?" Do you believe He is willing?

CHAPTER 9
OBEDIENCE AS A BACKBONE

"**N**ow Sarai, Abram's wife, had not been able to bear children for him. But she had an Egyptian servant named Hagar. *2* So Sarai said to Abram, "The Lord has prevented me from having children. Go and sleep with my servant. Perhaps I can have children through her." And Abram agreed with Sarai's proposal. *3* So Sarai, Abram's wife, took Hagar the Egyptian servant and gave her to Abram as a wife. (This happened ten years after Abram had settled in the land of Canaan.) So Abram had sexual relations with Hagar, and she became pregnant. But when Hagar knew she was pregnant, she began to treat her mistress, Sarai, with contempt. *5* Then Sarai said to Abram, "This is all your fault! I put my servant into your arms, but now that she's pregnant she treats me with contempt. The Lord will show who's wrong—you or me!"

Abram replied, "Look, she is your servant, so deal with her as you see fit." Then Sarai treated Hagar so harshly that she finally ran away. The angel of the Lord found Hagar beside a spring of water in the wilderness, along the road to Shur. *8* The angel said to her, "Hagar, Sarai's servant, where have you come from, and where are you going?" <u>"I'm running away from my mistress, Sarai," she replied.</u>

The angel of the Lord said to her, "Return to your mistress, and submit to her authority." Then he added, "I will give you more descendants than you can count." And the angel also said, "You are now pregnant and will give birth to a son. You are to name him Ishmael (which means 'God hears'), for the Lord has heard your cry of distress. This son of yours will be a wild man, as untamed as a wild donkey! He will raise his fist against everyone, and everyone will be against him. Yes, he will live in open hostility against all his relatives. Thereafter, Hagar used another name to refer to the Lord, who had spoken to her. She said, "You are the God who sees me."[a] She also said, "Have I truly seen the One who sees me?"

Genesis 16:1-13 (NLT)

Hagar was a servant who ran away when she was in the process of birthing something she didn't understand. When her situation became too hard her emotions let her run. But she made a choice to go back to what she tried running from which then allowed her to obtain the promise God had for her. *Hagar didn't compromise her obedience.*

REMEMBER WHY YOU STARTED

We never have to be concerned about something not working or something not going how we planned. If we are relying on our human hands then that means we are standing on our own skill-set instead of waiting on His timing with His hands. I learned that we do not have to clean up to show that we can be trusted. Why?

Because He's the kind of God who comes in and begins to pull back out all the mess we pushed in. Then sits down with us to say, 'That was thoughtful, but let's now go through this together.' It was then that I walked with Him through the different habits, the people, the relationships, all of it. And rather than my human hands picking up the wrong ones, He picked up the ones to be thrown away (the no's), the ones to be dusted off (the yes's), and the ones to be placed on the shelf (the not right now's). And I remember sitting in a gaze at my shelf, at my dustpan, and even at my trashcan.

And I remember I was certain that what it was, was good.
Because He is only good.

I read a quote once saying the only way to finish strong is to remember why you started. I have had that taped on my wall for years now. I believe the only way to keep moving at all, is to remember why you first started. When I moved back to Georgia, the home of bad memories and ache, I had no clue the hell I was walking into. All I knew is I heard the Lord say go, and something in me just had to. If anything didn't make sense, it was moving back to the church where I was kicked out of youth group at. The fact of the matter is that when you are listening to the quiet voice of the Holy Spirit and choosing to be obedient, the enemy is not going to play fair. The last thing the enemy wants is to see you respond the call of God on your life. Especially when you say yes even when it doesn't make sense to the human eye. Because I learned in those situations, where you really do look a little crazy because everything seems like its falling a part, those are the times where God gets the most glory and where God can show himself most true to you.

So here's Hagar. Pregnant with a promise from God. Because pregnancy is indeed a gift from Heaven above. Hagar didn't understand what all was going on inside of her. She didn't understand why she was the one to carry out this promise. It was uncomfortable. It was emotionally draining. Her surroundings were attacking her. All the while God was intentionally having her go through a specific process that would teach us a lesson to impact our lives forever. My two years that I spent at the College with the church I moved to in Georgia were hell on Earth. Honestly, I questioned why I was there almost everyday because of how uncomfortable my circumstances were. The only thing that kept my feet planted was the Lord telling me to stay. I worked everyday, cried more than twice a day, missed every event because I had to work, lost every relationship with my family, and felt as if I was never going to see the end.

It was an early Sunday morning in Spring, right after Daylight Savings. Pitch black outside and humid as can be. I had gotten home at two in the morning because of work and after three hours of sleep there I was at seven o'clock. Grabbing my Bible and notebook as I rushed out the door to try and beat the rain before I arrived to church. I opened the door to my black 1998, vehicle with spray paint on the passengers door, a sunroof that was stuck half way open, no air conditioning and a cracked engine. I didn't have to worry about unlocking the door, because the locks were broken, too.

My car started bouncing it's way to church when I felt a drop of rain on my forehead. I knew it was downhill from there. Before I had a chance for a backup plan, I looked like I had just taken a shower. Which was partially in my favor because then at least you couldn't tell if the drops on my face were from tears or from raindrops. But I'll never forget in the midst of how seemingly hurtful that morning was, I started singing an old hymn. And I am not a singer. But I made myself worship. As much as I didn't understand. As much as I was hurting. As tired as I was and as confused as I was, I chose to praise my way through. Like David in majority of the Psalms, I had to learn and understand what it meant to praise in the storm. David understood that God is not a God who waits to meet you when you get OUT of the storm.

More-so, He is a gracious God who is waiting to meet you IN the storm. And when we learn how to praise IN the storm only then will we see our way OUT of the storm. I know it firsthand that we spend a lot of time waiting on God but sometimes, He's the one waiting on us to lift our hands. He's waiting to see if our praise is authentic or if our praise is conditional on our circumstance. I had to choose to believe that eventually, the storm has to run out of rain. My prayer is that we wouldn't be a people who wait until it runs out to lift our hands to praise.

There will be times that are so aching and there will be times where your emotions will run you dry. There will be times, in the middle of you being used by God that it becomes too much to handle. There will come a time where the Lord forming and creating such a miraculous gifting inside of us to the point where it's actually so big that it scares us in our own humanness. Like Hagar, there may come a point where we throw the towel in and sprint away from our circumstance and call a quits.

But notice in verse 8.

The angel said to her, "Hagar, Sarai's servant, where have you come from, and where are you going?"

The angel reminded Hagar where she came from. Reminded Hagar of why she started. People don't run away from their promise because they're awful sinners or bad people. No, they run because life has a way of happening so hard that they forget why they started. Which then causes people to lose sight of where they were headed. Life has a way of hurting us so deeply and in some seasons, isolating us so strongly where there really does not seem as if there is a purpose to keep moving. Almost as if we're in the middle of the ocean alone and all there is around us is deep waters.

In my second year of college in Georgia, after I made it through the first year of crying days on end and working every free minute there was I found life hitting me in my gut once again. Still listening to God and staying planted where He placed me life really gave me a battle where I had every logical reason to throw up the peace sign and dip out. Within two years, I had moved seven times and all of which were out of my control entirely. This one particular time that drove me to my knees was when my parents had actually moved up to Georgia. My relationship with my mom was rocky but they wanted me to move in with them. There was a student who was is need of housing so I gave up my spot in apartment a few months into my lease and let her take my spot and I moved in with my parents. Six weeks in after getting everything settled I was at church on a Wednesday night and we were on a church-wide fast. In 2017 I was dating this guy who I'll talk about later on and that night I felt the Lord prompting me to break up and walk away from the relationship. I had felt off the entirety of the relationship but as I'll mention later on, this man was my security in the midst of all the chaos in my life.

My bones couldn't shake this prompting so I called him immediately after service and he was not the most receptive so we agreed to go on a break. Which might I add, if you feel like you're suppose to put an end to something then put an end to it. Don't compromise and don't beat around the bush. It may be terrifying but the comforting part? *The Lord calls us to obedience. He doesn't call us to have the perfect strategy in the aftermath.* He just wants our trust.

So, I broke off really the only thing that was supporting me in this season and instantly the feeling of loneliness and uncertainty flooded my mind because I didn't know what would be next. The very next day I was out with a friend and I get a call from my mom. In this time she never agreed with me being here doing what I was doing and I remember her just shouting and repeating all the things I heard throughout my first year. "You never should have came here." "You aren't suppose to be here." "You are meant to be in Florida, not here." "God isn't in this."

Tirelessly, tears flooded my face because it was hard enough as it was and to not have the support by your own mother creates an emptiness that nothing can really fill. At the end of that conversation, she proceeded to tell me she was kicking me out and she was already back on her way to Florida. I had no idea what on Earth I was going to do. We were on a fast. I was obedient to the Lord in breaking off the relationship and then next day my mom leaves and kicks me out. What the heck? I thought fasting is when the Lord is suppose to bless us and do all of these incredible things. Right? That's what I thought. In my own humanness and in a panic of not knowing what to do, I called the boyfriend who I just broke up with and he came and helped me move all of my things to his house because I had nowhere to go. I made my trunk in my car my closet and for a few weeks I hopped from friends house to friends house and lived out of my car. There was this one week, my dad had moved back to Florida with my mom but they still had the house they were renting in Georgia. And I'll never forget the nights of leaving work at two in the morning and going to this empty house with just a mattress in one of the bedrooms. All alone. Theoretically, pregnant with a promise from God trying to pursue this call of God on my life.

I think Hagar felt alone, too. Notice that after Hagar was reminded of where she came from, and where she was going, she chose to go back to what she tried running from. My friend, sometimes, it's going to take us humbling ourselves and returning back to what we first ran from. This could even be something we tried running from ten years ago, and the Lord has been waiting on us to go back. Because taking steps back, does not always been you're behind. Rather, taking steps back prepares to propel you forward at a much more rapid speed than you would be if you kept moving as you were. It was when Hagar remembered where she came from, and why she started that she was able to obtain the promise that the Lord had for her.

REMEMBER WHOSE YOU ARE

It is not difficult to make decisions when you know what you value. It's evident that Hagar was moved by the voice of God that she chose to go back, therefore proved she valued what God had for her. Here's the thing. If it takes your attention, it's not worth it. This can be people, relationships, friendships, addictions, habits, and even thought patterns.

"In all your ways acknowledge him, and he will make straight your paths. Be not wise in your own eyes; fear the Lord, and turn away from evil. it will be healing to your flesh and refreshment to your bones." Proverbs 3:6-8 (ESV)

What can we classify as evil? Anything that would take our attention off of Him. "Turn away" in the original text literally means to turn off. Meaning to refuse acceptance to, to send away, to reject. So what this is saying... is to reject anything that may take our attention off of Him, even if it be for a moment. And this will be the core and the backbone in our influence.

Hagar made a choice that though her emotions were shouting at her it's not worth it to stay, she had the ability to shut it down. And only she had that ability. In my experiences, I have learned that nobody can determine what our values are except for us. Everyone can speak into what they think should be important to us and everybody loves trying to decide what the right path is for us. But when it comes down to it, we are the only one who has the honor of choosing what is going to hold value in our life.

It's easy to let our circumstances shape our beliefs and even hinder what we thought was important to us. It's inevitable that at times, we may disengage ourselves with our core values. We may shift our beliefs to fill the empty spaces we encounter, and we may even drop our beliefs based off the pain we have experienced from carrying them in the first place. I believe that is what Hagar encountered. She knew what was important to her but her circumstance was so heavy it was shoving her values beneath her. But she made a choice to rise up against her flesh and listen to what the Lord was saying. Even when it didn't make sense.

Going back for Hagar was undoubtably awkward, but she didn't owe an explanation to anybody other than the Lord. And don't owe explanations either. You don't have to defend your steps anymore. You don't have to hesitate to be great. It's okay for you to be you. In a meek way with a side of confidence. To be you in your fullest capacity. Do that. No longer should anyone hold back because we don't want people to think we are all that. No longer should we allow inadequacy to make its home at our doorstep. You are a leader of yourself, and the people around us.

You see, notice how traffic signs relate so heavily in our human lives and detect a lot of different seasons we get to go through. Not sure about you, but I've been in seasons where there were stop signs, dead end signs, and curvy road ahead signs all around me (which doesn't mean I always noticed them). However, in this season I found myself at one point with a yield sign in front of me. To yield literally means to give way to the pressure. To yield means you are not able to stop and you are not able to turn around. To yield means you aren't really prepared for what's ahead but you know that you just have to keep moving. And I feel like we all get to a place in our lives where we obtain the deep understanding that we don't have the option to turn around and where we don't have the option to stop moving.

We get to a place where God has already allowed us to pass and move on from all of the 'Do Not Enter' and 'Stop' signs and we find ourselves coming up to this moment of having no other option other than to keep moving forward. We get to this place and get a glimpse of the oncoming traffic and we glance back and see the people behind us. And in this moment we get two choices. We can stop or we can keep moving. Being fully aware that if we were to completely stop and slam on our breaks then we ultimately would damage the people behind us who are following us. And if we were to speed forward as fast as we can attempting to avoid collision, we ultimately would damage the people we're about to come in contact with.

> No matter how uncomfortable.
> No mater how saddening.
> No matter how hurtful.
> No matter how scary.
> No matter how unusual.

Keep moving. Whether it's paralyzing stillness or unfathomable joy. Keep moving. Hidden blessings or tender pruning. Keep moving. Regardless of whatever is ahead may look like to our human eyes. *Keep moving.*

It won't always make sense. Sometimes, it's going to be real hard. But I believe if we allow ourselves to give way even a tiny bit to what God is trying to do then I believe and rest in the holy truth that we're in good hands. He's well worth trusting. You are an influencer. And I beg for you to walk that out. No more pasts, no more insecurities, and no more doubts. Go all in. The Lord has too much planned for you to sit back and contemplate the day you want to speak up.

Start today, I promise you have a whole lot of people rooting for you. Because here's a secret, like Hagar, speaking up can be done without words, too. Sometimes, speaking up is just getting up and silently going back to what you value. And more times than you think, that is louder than anything you could have spoken.

HONEST TRUTH

"Meanwhile, the moment we get tired in the waiting, God's Spirit is right along-side helping us along. If we don't know how or what to pray, it doesn't matter. He does our praying in and for us, making prayer out of our wordless sighs, our aching groans. He knows us far better than we know ourselves, knows our pregnant condition, and keeps us present before God. That's why we can be so sure that every detail in our lives of love for God is worked into something good."

Romans 8:28 (MSG)

CHALLENGE

Often enough, He is trying to create something new. Let's refuse to ignore His nudges and hints. Let's refuse to be so caught up in what SEEMS right that we miss out on what IS right. Let's refuse to let our human tendencies triumph over His spirit leading us. Let's refuse to silence His directions because our thoughts are trying to shout louder. He is God and He is only good.

Let's trust Him.

REFLECTION

I.   What does obedience mean to you?

II. Why did you start doing what you're doing?

III. Has there been a time where you feel like the Lord told you to go somewhere or do something that didn't make any sense? Did you listen? What was the outcome?

IV. What is the scariest part of blindly listening to what you feel the Lord is telling you? Have you ever regretted listening to Him?

V.   Who have you learned God to be by listening to the things you did not understand? How has this changed your concept of God?

CHAPTER 10

INTUITION AS A CONFIDENCE

"When many of his disciples heard it, they said, "This is a hard saying; who can listen to it?" But Jesus, knowing in himself that his disciples were grumbling about this, said to them, "Do you take offense at this? Then what if you were to see the Son of Man ascending to where he was before? It is the Spirit who gives life; the flesh is no help at all. The words that I have spoken to you are spirit and life. But there are some of you who do not believe." (For Jesus knew from the beginning who those were who did not believe, and who it was who would betray him.) And he said, "This is why I told you that no one can come to me unless it is granted him by the Father."

After this many of his disciples turned back and no longer walked with him. So Jesus said to the twelve, "Do you want to go away as well?" Simon Peter answered him, "Lord, to whom shall we go? You have the words of eternal life, and we have believed, and have come to know, that you are the Holy One of God."

John 6:60-69 (ESV)

Peter was the one who watched everyone walk away from Jesus and had a choice to walk away, too. But Peter was the one who had the wide-eyed recognition of where he came from and where he was going. And in that moment he knew that there was absolutely nowhere else he'd rather be other than with Jesus. Peter knew he could go back to everything came from, but I imagine with tear filled eyes him looking at Jesus saying, "Where else would I go other than with you?" *Peter didn't compromise his intuition.*

YOU WALKED AWAY ONCE, TOO

The disciples hear a message by Jesus that would gain very little popularity in the church today. A call to leave it all, to lay it all down, to risk it all, to abandon the known for the unknown. And many in the crowd walk away. It's funny because we all do our little church gasp when we read that people actually walked away from Jesus. But really, do we blame them? We walked away with them for years, leaving the commands of Jesus in the distance. Years after deciding to follow Jesus many of us find ourselves in the same position, still hearing the same sermon, to abandon all.

So, let's talk about my man Peter. If there is anyone I relate to most it's Peter. He just kept falling on his face time after time. And I'm just like, I get you, Peter. Because me, too. Peter was the man who denied Jesus. We know that. But I like to classify Peter as human. Because we all have denied Jesus in some way, shape, or form. Whether it be with our words, actions, or even thoughts. We've done it.

We read in verse 60, *"This is a hard saying; who can listen to it?"*

This was not something hard to understand, but hard to accept. The word for 'hard' originally means 'dry,' and 'rough;' and then in a moral sense, 'offensive.' (If they were offended way back in the day, Lord knows how people get offended today.) "Who can hear" actually means who can submit to listen to it? Who can submit to listen to something that is essentially going to uncomfortably and radically change the entirety of their lives? Disciples start grumbling,

"What the heck"
"I have a party to go to next week"
"Life is hard enough as it is, I'm not going to make myself that entirely different."
"Im a good person as I am, I don't need that"

In their own humanness they talked in a low tone so that He could not hear but the Bible says Jesus knew without hearing. To get to the Father, essentially it takes more than normality. You can't get to the Father looking like everybody else. You can't get to the Father with a blunt in your hand and a bottle in the other. You can't get to the Father if from the bird eye perspective, no one can see you because you are merely blending in with the rest of the world.

In verse 65, it states *"After this many of his disciples turned back and no longer walked with him."* The Greek expresses more context than the English. They went away (ἀπό) apo, means *"away from,"* from Christ. Literally, to the things behind. To what they had left in the beginning to follow the Lord. In today's world, I have the deep understanding of the struggle between blending in and standing out. When we say yes to Jesus, we say no to the lifestyle the world praises. It's not always easy. I will never tell somebody following Jesus is easy. Because it's not easy when everybody you know is going out drinking and you're sitting at home with a book. It's not easy when everybody is bashing somebody and you're battling with yourself on whether to stay silent, stick up for the person, or join in. It's not easy when life is shattering right in front of your face and all you want to do is go out for a drink or get in the bed with somebody to take your mind off of real life struggles. And we all have struggled with these thoughts because we are all human. Even following Jesus, we are still human and we still are going to have thoughts we are going to need to stand against. We're foolish if we think that is not the case.

If we aren't in love with Jesus then why in the world would we want to keep our lives pure? When we don't know Jesus all of these requests for purity seem like rules. When we don't know Jesus, all of the scripture on not getting drunk seem crazy. When we don't know Jesus, every commandment sounds whack. But when we fall in love with ruler, then it's our hearts desire to follow the rules. And don't get my words twisted. Following Jesus is not rules and regulations. My gosh. Following Jesus is understanding his heart for us and everything he lays out for us to follow is for our own good. The commandments aren't whack. Humans are whack.

THE DANGER OF PONDERING

If I could sum up my life in my early years of walking with the Lord, the one word it would sit firmly as is 'contradiction.' The entirety of every one of my important relationships has exploded with contradiction. Saying one thing but doing another. Going back on their word and never coming to pass with it. Flooding out words they never meant from their mouth simply because it sounded good. Lovers, friends, family too.

Maybe it's because we're human. I don't know all the answers but I have learned that people will hurt us. And there isn't a thing that we can do about it. I use to think that not being able to give practical advice in hard circumstances was just me being 'too Christian.' But really, the only thing that keeps me sane is reliance on God. With all that goes on in life I shrink at the thought of being unaware of a God who is constant. Because with Him, He stomps on contradiction and He uplifts consistency.

If you have followed along with me me then you know generally, I try to keep the overly spiritual talk out of my blogs because I don't believe that you have to always pump up spirituality for people to know you love the Lord. I am a huge fan of practicality and I love relevancy in topics of life. But when it comes to a day by day basis, knowing God is the one thing that keeps me going. He's the one thing that has proved himself true, even when it's been a billion years later than what I wanted. When He speaks, it sits well within my soul. Because it's always honest.

I look at it like this. In our life we're given this canvas and overtime we proudly paint what we want our life to look like on it. And when we let someone close to us, we freely give them the brush. And more often than most, they don't choose to paint on it until heartache. So here we are carrying around our canvas of what we have made for ourselves and what other people have put on us - and then there's God. Up there with our canvas that He has freshly painted for us. And the funny thing is, He's just chilling and patiently waiting for us to ask for an exchange that He's always faithful to give.

I use to think that I was okay with just slipping into church here and there when I felt down. I had the mindset that life in and of itself was just contradicting, no way around it. I would see these people who's lives revolved around God and who always seemed to be happy and it would make me cringe. Because I didn't get it. But now I understand that just because those people always seemed happy - didn't mean that they were happy. Rather, I have experienced for myself that I am so human. So so so human and I am not happy all the time. Sometimes, I would love to trip back up in my old habits and call it a quits. Sometimes, I say things way too quickly that should not have been said. Sometimes, everything that's important to me falls to pieces and I'm left sitting in silence. Sometimes, really human things happen.

In spite of all that, I can have my head lifted up and seemingly look happy because I know a God who gets me. I know a God who is getting ready to hand me a new canvas with His personal painting on it. Who doesn't mind the dozen of scuffed up canvases I've been carrying. The brilliant thing about God - is that He beautifully floods us with certainty that we could never find anywhere else. And seeking that everyday? It pulls everything into perspective for our really human life. It was one of

Peter's sweetest proclamations - out of a passionate heart and of an authentic love. There was no one else who could show him the right way.

His response spoke, "You are my God. On the mountain and in the valley. You were the God at the beginning and you are the God at the end. You are where every hungry soul finds a meal. Where every tired soul finds a place of rest. There isn't any other than you. In you there is grace and direction. In you there is security from every enemy. Who else is there other than you?"

Simon Peter answered, "You are the Messiah, the Son of the living God."
Matthew 16:16 (NLT)

Was Peter perfect? Ha! No! But he had his eyes set unto what mattered to him. He had his heart in alignment with the heart of God. He got up when he fell down. He spent time with Jesus. Peter understood that the love of God is what frees us *from* sin not what frees us *to* sin. He spent time with Jesus to know the very of heart of God which is why he knew he could go back to the old relationships. He knew he could back to the self doubt. He could go back to the normality of his life, to the parties, to the unhealthy habits. He could watch as EVERYONE was walking away. These people were probably his friends and when it made sense to walk away with them, too, his response set the standard for Christianity today.

Peter knew the heart of God and so he chose to remain planted in what he knew what true. He didn't leave room to ponder. He didn't leave room to allow his mind and his own human logic to make a decision for him. When a life altering question was asked to Peter with every set of eyes watching him, he didn't have to go off and pray about what was the right choice. He was rooted in the truth of who Jesus was and who he was in

Jesus. Therefor when the question was asked, "Do you want to walk away, too?" He knew without a shadow of a doubt who Jesus was and where he stood.

And with weary hands and a heavy heart I hope our heart repeats the same words he did. "Where else would I go?" In our weakest moments I hope we still look at Jesus and with tear filled eyes choose to stand with Him knowing full well there is absolutely no place else we would rather be.

A PASSIONATE HEART MATTERS

It's the patterns of a heart that will always gleam through the spaces in a mask. My heart had become more aware to look through that space before accepting a front that has been made. A wise soul once said, 'Step back and just take a seat. a mask is only wearable for a short season, much like an occasion.' And that struck something in my backbone. I think we can all agree that humanity is really good at being human. And as the disciples who walked away, there has been this unremitting desire to be somebody we are not in order to keep something that we want.

Here's what I'm learning everyday — when the human heart attempts to reconstruct who they are for another human, it's not sustainable. I've seen it firsthand, that heart will throw away the mask and will always end up sprinting back to it's original form. I've been the one to throw the mask away and I've been the one to see the mask thrown away. But here's the quietly wise thing about God and His creativity in constructing the human life. Sitting back, I have seen how character always makes its way to the spotlight, whether the heart wants it to or not. And character doesn't show up dressed head to toe with a fresh cut and new kicks. Character pushes to the front inherently raw as it is. It leaves the mask, it leaves the crowd, and it shows up proud and tall.

Character outshines occasion. Character can be hidden for a short period — but character knows it is important enough to be seen. I hope we can become brave enough to remove our own mask, and bold enough take a step back from the people who are not willing to remove theirs. I hope when it makes the headline, it is something noteworthy. Something admirable. Something uncommon, in a holy way.

HONEST TRUTH

"The wise counsel God gives when I'm awake
  is confirmed by my sleeping heart.
Day and night I'll stick with God;
  I've got a good thing going and I'm not letting go.
I'm happy from the inside out,
  and from the outside in, I'm firmly formed.
You canceled my ticket to hell—
  that's not my destination!
Now you've got my feet on the life path,
  all radiant from the shining of your face.
Ever since you took my hand,
  I'm on the right way."

Psalm 16:8-11 (MSG)

CHALLENGE

God does not withhold out of spite.
God does not withhold without a purpose.
God does not withhold to make us ache.
In fact —
God withholds because He sees it is good.
God withholds with a holy purpose.
God withholds so we do not ache in the long run.

Let's ditch the idea that we are missing out because He is withholding something that we think we want.

Let's stop engaging and entertaining the things (people, places, jobs, actions, and thoughts) that God is not in.

REFLECTION

I.   What were your first thoughts when you were introduced to Jesus and what it meant to be a disciple of Christ? Did it freak you out? Why or why not?

II. In what ways do you find yourself relating to Peter? Do you feel Peter is a good example for us to look to? In what ways, yes or no?

III. How do you differentiate your emotions and what Holy Spirit is trying to tell you? Have you ever been mistaken? How did you deal with that?

IV. Can you go back to a time where you walked away? Why do you think you did? What did walking away before shape in you now?

V.   What makes you passionate about Jesus? How can this passion introduce people to him?

CHAPTER 11
YOUR MINISTRY DESERVED THAT BREAK UP

Leadership first and foremost is laying compromise at the altar.
Then recognizing that once you lay it down, it is not yours to pick back up.

THEY'RE WORTH IT

I am forever thankful that I lived through every moment, and every
feeling of 2018. That was the year I fell in love with my Winter season and
watched as I allowed it to change the course of my entire life. I watched as
each event instilled new deep-rooted standards in my soul. 2018 breathed
grace and it breathed fire.

Why do we entertain things God is not in? Okay. Once again, I'm
sorry if I stepped on your toes with this one. Kind of, but not really
though. Because I wish someone with honest eyes told me this one earlier
on. For me, before knowing the Lord, I spent the time that I was in relationships with boys who later on in life ended up in jail. Not because they
were bad people by any means, but because they had no vision for their
lives at the time. As I mentioned earlier on, I don't believe in 'bad people'. I
believe in lost people. Because I was one, too. So, after being single for the
four years I spent in ministry school, when I met someone who actually
seemed like they had their life in order it was like, "Oh wow, hey there."
And I know this is so your typical Christian response, but hear me. Just because it is good does not mean it is God. I promise that the still small voice
we hear in our heart holds more power than we give it credit.

In the muggy Summer air, I stepped out of my black 1998, vehicle
I talked about earlier. My shirt was stained with flour and I had marinara
sauce on my brown sneakers that use to be white because I had just gotten
off work at a local pizza shop. I served as a waitress and it was one of my
three jobs I had been working at the time. There I was. Nineteen. In Geor-

gia all by myself blindly following this call of God I felt on my life. Knowing I had been called to full time ministry and to preach the un-compromised Word of God, my life seemingly looked the complete opposite. The towing company was on my speed dial because every car I had kept breaking down to the point where I had to pay and use one of those car services to pick me up and take me to each of my jobs.

We hear many times the saying of girls having, "Daddy Issues", however in my case, I had mommy issues. Deep issues, too. Every girl desires her mom to be her biggest fan and best friend. To know her mom is by her side to keep her standing tall in every season. To know that at the end of the day if everyone else rejects her then she can always lean back on her mom to accept her. In this season of my life, I was drowning in the disapproval of my mom and suffocating in her disownment. Day in and day out her words would shatter my soul of telling me God wouldn't ever use me in Georgia. Day in and day out how I was a fool for thinking otherwise. Eventually, I learned boundaries are essential to put up, even for family. I learned God's yes always triumphs mans opinion.

So there I was in the muggy Summer air, stepping out of my car to get gas. With all of the chaos in my life, this boy pulled up in this expensive car to the pump next to my trap car (wasn't really a trap car, but it sure could pass as one). We ended up speaking and exchanging phone numbers. Why did I give my number to a boy at a Gas Station? I don't know but I do know you shouldn't follow in my footsteps for that one. One of our first times hanging out he told me we were going to the lake. So I put on a thrifted t-shirt with a hole in it and ripped up jean shorts. He picked me up and took me to his moms house, which was a houseboat, and we were actually going to the Mayor's houseboat for a party first.

Looking homeless, I walked up into the Mayor's houseboat to meet everyone looking like a hot mess while they were all dressed up eating their fancy hors d'oeuvres. Him and his family were well off and I so was well not. Welcome to the typical life of struggles with Hope. Shortly after, we began to pursue a relationship. Before I move any further, let me tell you, if you are not in prayer diligently seeking the Lord before you say yes to a relationship then do not enter into a relationship. He was a great person. Really. He knew of God, but he was not in love with God. There's a big difference. He came into my life at a time where hell was breaking lose and in a lot of ways, showed up for me in ways I was not capable of to show up for myself. I believe there is purpose in all things and though he was not right for me, the Lord allowed him to play a part in my story. However, I learned money does not buy love and money does not keep love. Do not try and convince yourself otherwise.

I journal everyday. I have since I was seventeen. If you read my journal entries from the day I met him, you would read how I wrote I knew he wasn't right. How he was good, but how I knew it was not God. This is the boyfriend who I went on a break with during the fast in 2017. For a year, I wrote almost everyday how I was not in love and how I knew God was calling me out but I felt so stuck. How I felt so pressured because of all of the eyes watching my every step. At this point, the Lord proved himself faithful, as He always does, and I was hired full-time for the ministry school I moved back to Georgia to attend. I ended up working for the church that I was kicked out of youth. Dropping out of High School and now working as one of the ministry school directors. Pastor Blake, the one who kicked me out, ended up being my boss five years later and his family became like my own. How crazy is God? The church my mom paid me to attend was now paying me to work.

But in this season, I held it with honor that I had a hundred students with innocent eyes watching my every step as their leader. If you know that the Lord is not giving you the go ahead to pursue something, LISTEN to it. And put action towards it, too. Do not try and convince yourself that you can handle it. Because here's the thing. God cares about us so much that when it's all said and done, He will absolutely have the final say. Graciously, yet adamantly. Our human hands can only hold onto something we are not meant to hold for so long. Do yourself the favor and put it down now. We can't have the mindset, "Eventually I will."

A Pastor who I look up to named Robert, told me whatever we say can happen eventually, needs to happen immediately. And that small statement changed my entire life. Months passed and we had been dating just over a year. I was twenty and working in my dream at the ministry school. In the midst of me shoving what I knew the Lord was planting on my heart under the rug, and choosing comfortability over calling, he proposed.

Everything seemed so good from the surface so how could I say no? He was financially stable and took care of me. He would come to church with me and try to lead us spiritually. He was a kind hearted person. But something in my spirit was fighting so frantically to get out and I flat out ignored it. I knew the day after I hesitantly said yes to the ring that was now on my finger that I was wrong and I was desperate for the Lord to do a work in me. Though there were many things not in alignment with the Lord in his life, it would be easy for me to push all the blame on him. But I would be foolish to tell you it was all him. I was very broken and unsteady because of everything that was going on in my life.

I sure did love the Lord, but my heart was exhausted from the never-ending events in my life I was not even capable to love myself healthy.

Let alone another human being. So there I was, twenty and engaged. Leading a ministry college with not a clue of what I was doing and really, not a clue of who I was anymore. I will never forget the day we went to pre-marital counseling. Our counselor, Andy, was the same counselor who counseled me when I was fifteen, so he knew the real Hope. We sat down and he knew. Andy had him step out of the room and I will never forget him leaning forward in his chair and looking at my eyes saying, "You're not in this, are you?"

Tears ran down my face and my head just shook. Pastor Blake and his wife, Laura, have always told me that tears express what words cannot. And I had never had something designate so deeply than I did in that moment. How does someone who is suppose to lead the way of a hundred students watching her break off an engagement that looks perfect from the outside? How was I suppose to tell him and everybody that it was over after we already sent out invitations and I had already bought a dress? How was I going to make this decision not knowing the influence I might lose from these students watching me? Won't I look inconsistent? Won't I look like I didn't hear from God? Won't I look like I'm not someone they should be following?

Talk about pressure. I was terrified. But, I learned firsthand what I will share till the day I go home. You are never too far in to take a step back. After it was all said and done, I realized that I cared more about the call of God on my life than I did about opinions or even feelings. But that was a choice that no one else could make for me. In this time one of my closest friends had just moved to Georgia. I count him as family. After years of not seeing each other we met up for coffee and I shared with him briefly about what was going on and he said something that really drew the final line for me.

He looked at me across the table after listening to me rant and he said five words that I have carried with me to this day, "*Your ministry deserves this break-up.*" If you know me and my dramatic self, I sat in disbelief with my mouth wide open as if that was the most profound statement I had ever heard in my life. But realized how accurate he was. The people we are leading and the people we are going to lead one day deserve us to break up with anything that may hinder us now.

Regardless of who's watching or what your position is, I promise you I know on this one, you aren't too far in to take a step back. My students deserved that break up. Why? For the reason because God was not in it, I was hindering myself from being able to be my most effective self. For me, it was a physical break up. But from my physical break up, I dug deeper and began to recognize the habits I needed to break up with. Then I recognized the vocabulary I needed to break up with. Then I dug really deep and saw the thought patterns I had to break up with. Sometimes, it's a physical break up. Other times, it's deeper than that. When I finally decided to break up with humankind, that's when it clicked. When I decided to grab the hand of the One who made me, rather than the hands of the ones who were trying to make me. I found that I blossomed with His hand holding me, rather than with the hands that tried pushing me.

If God's not in it, I don't want it.
The people you're leading deserve for you to have this mentality.

YOU'RE WORTH IT

You are meant to compliment somebody, not change somebody

If you're anything like me then sometimes, we bravely hold on tight to our flawed propositions. Standing tall behind thoughts that we tell our heart to be true. Reality can be screaming in our face with evidence that can't be argued and we sit there with our eyes squeezed shut as if our simple hope subdues the truth in existence - not everyone is kind. I'm a firm believer in overlooking indecency to get a glimpse of the human heart. A firm believer that when we walk into a room full of faces we're all wanting of the same thing, acceptance. I believe in the depths of every heart there's gold even if it's surrounded by ash. There's always gold. But the paralyzing truth I have peeked my eye open to see - not everyone is kind. And the gracious certainty I have painted on the walls of my home - everyone can be kind.

Just because everyone can be kind, doesn't mean everyone is kind. And just because you want to be everybody's number one fan, doesn't mean you should be. In my own life, I have chased more than what I was capable of and I have made rooms in my heart to seat many people who never stayed for coffee, only for a short meal. Often, I think about all the feet that have walked out of the rooms in my heart and I catch myself keeping count of how many times I heard the door shut one by one. But what I have learned, slowly, is that it doesn't matter who's walked out of the room. The predominant beauty is who still is in the room. Not everyone is kind, so be careful with who you rearrange your space for. Yes, I'm a BIG believer in there being good in every soul. But you can't bring people close holding onto the expectation of the kindness you believe to see in them. You, yourself, be kind. Welcome everyone with a smile but not everyone with a seat. You can believe the best while being standing wise.

I want to make this one plain and simple. It's not our job to instill our morals into somebody else. It is not our place to drill our values into somebody else. It is not even in our ability to create a lasting change in somebody. Because I've seen firsthand that they'll go right back to what you had them turn away from once we're out of the picture.

It's not our job to mold someone into the person we want so that they can be compatible with us. We spend too much time searching for someone who is teachable rather than searching for God and waiting for Him to give us someone who He has already completed. It's our job to seek the Lord. It's our place to focus on ourselves to be the best that we can be. It's our job to let the Lord in to create a lasting change in us. It's our job to strive for Him and wait for someone who is striving for Him, too. Not wait on someone to play catch up to us. Just slow down. He's got you. And if you knew what He was preparing for you, you wouldn't mind waiting.

You're worth waiting for God's best for you. You don't have to try and create something out of potential of how good it could be. Potential is not always praise worthy. Potential is almost always a hard let down because we fall in love the hopeful potential instead of understanding the current reality. You're worth waiting for God's best. In relationships, in jobs, in everything. Usually when we choose to wait for God's best it pushes us to take the step to let go of something that is sub-par. Sometimes, He'll ask us to let go of something that we don't view as sub-par and it can really put us at a crossroads. Our human eyes believe we know what we need and when we are asked to let go of it we can find ourselves in a panic. But here's the thing.

When God asks us to let go of something the question is not,
"What am I going to miss out on if I let this go?"
The real question is,
"What am I going to miss out on if I don't let this go?"

This one hits home because the Lord so tenderly laid this on my heart one night. I think so often when the Lord is tugging on us to release something, our first human response is "But God.. What if I miss ___ ?"

Man oh man. God is so incredibly wise to know what we do not. If we switch the perspective on this and take it off of ourselves, the question becomes, "Oh God..What am I going to miss if I don't let this go?" We need to understand the Lord never takes what He doesn't intend to exchange. Trust that the Lord knows what He's doing. He'll prompt us to do something, but it then rests on our decision if we do it or not. Which is why I believe we are a product of our decisions not our circumstance.

Our circumstances don't destroy us. Our decisions do.

We choose what we do with what is given us. And we choose what we do with what is asked of us. We can doom in what it is, or we can celebrate it for what it is. I choose to celebrate. Because I have really, really learned that whatever the case may be — it's good. In some way, shape, or form it is going to be good. Because He is good. And that is the raw and inherent truth.

You know what else is inherently true? White shoes are unreasonably grueling to keep clean. I mean, really.

They're suppose to remain without scuffs but the fact that they are going to get dirty is inevitable. I clean them, then they get dirty, and I lean them again. But I don't ever throw them away when they get a few scuffs. I wash them because I don't mind. I wash them because I paid a price for them. I wash them because they are mine. Call me whack, but I think this relates to our relationship with God on such a weighty level. We go about our lives striving to be the best we can for Him, and time to time we trip and scrape our knee. And other times, we fall and break our leg. We all develop a few stains over time and end up not being as whole-some as we ought to be. Being human, it's inevitable.

But when it comes down to it, all we have to do is get real with God and say, "Hey, it's me... I got a little scuffed up again." And He's going to look at us with a big ole smirk and say, "I know... now let me clean you up again." Why? Because scuffs don't intimidate God. Because we're His and He paid a price for us. Because He loves to see us whole and He's so able of doing so.

You're worth saying no to the average so you can say yes to the best.
You're worth knowing your boundaries and removing people who don't honor them.
You're worth stomping on the enemy's head with praise when he's acting like a fool.
You're worth reserving yourself for the Lord until He brings you the right one.
You're worth setting yourself apart from the secular patterns of the world.
You're worth letting yourself go through the refining process.
You're worth the wait.
You're worth the best.

HE'S WORTH IT

Sometimes God's healing looks a lot like hurting.

This. How quietly clever is God that he would use ache to be our gain. What a holy irony that is. It's been the seasons that I clenched on for dear life that I will never stop hanging on the walls of my house. The seasons of discomfort, and reconstructing. The seasons of pulling back out everything we once shoved in. The seasons of clearing the stage to where it was just us, and God. Those seasons. Those are the ones that serve as a welcome mat to the people we meet. Love those seasons. Embrace those seasons. Heal from those seasons, and turn around to use those seasons.

For me, I had a very broken family for majority of my life. There was a time where I didn't talk to any of my family members other than my parents for seven years. There was a time where my mom and I would only talk here and there for years. To this day, I haven't seen two of my brothers in over twelve years and I haven't seen one of my aunts in over fifteen years. Family has always been a touchy subject for me and for a long time I believed that I was made to do this life by myself and that family would not be something that I had until I was married with kids.

In my last relationship, for the short moment when I thought that was going to be my future, I was really disappointed in God for a season. None of his family knew the Lord, and we spent months of not speaking to them because every time I'd come around his sisters would be so hateful. They all thought I was crazy and would tell me how I wasn't a real Christian. It was so draining. Coming from a broken family, and then stepping into a family that was broken was the cherry on top. I knew in my heart that it wasn't suppose to be like that and I knew the Lord had quietly promised me a family. A God-fearing, healthy family. A family that would reshape my view on what family is. That alone was worth it for me to wait for.

For three years I spent every Thanksgiving and Christmas by myself. It was my new normal. To this day holidays still sting a little because when have a past similar to mine it's this weird in between where you don't really know where you belong. But over time I actually started to look forward to the holidays. You see, every holiday I started a tradition with myself. Since I didn't have family to spend it with, I would drive down to Atlanta and find the homeless people who didn't have family to spend the day with either. Looking back, probably not my wisest decision to stroll the streets of Atlanta by myself. However, I would meet the greatest people every time and I wouldn't change it for the world. Some of the people you meet really are sweetest gifts and not your stereotypical homeless people that we make them out to be. They're all people with a story that is worth hearing. And I am so honored that I have been able to hear them. Circumstances only break us if we choose to let circumstances break us. He's worth it for us to choose otherwise. Because His plans are always for us to prosper. He's faithful. He's true. He's constant. I don't know what in your life needs to be broken up with, but I will tell you He's worth it.

Here's a popular topic of conversation even though we all pretend we don't ask these questions:

'How can you tell if you're with the right person?'
'How do you know if it's true?'
'How are sure that it's right?'

If you've thought one of these, raise your hand because I have, too.

There have been seasons in my life where I was desperately pleading for answers in each of these questions and here's what I learned once I hit the bottom. To first know love - you first have to know Him. And I mean really know Him. I'm telling you, hitting the bottom teaches you what you would never learn on the top. And that's why I believe understanding love and knowing God go hand in hand.

Many of us have known many types of love throughout our lives but the one that has come out on top of every aching time is this one. Right? And what got me was when I noticed that there was never a time of convincing myself that I was in love with this Jesus.

This love was not something that I had to try to do or make myself do.
This love was not something that made me feel pressured.
This love was not something that drowned me in doubt.
This love was not something that left me angry more than it did at peace.
This love was not something that made me question who i was.

But this love was sure without question and it was certain.
This love screamed selfless, in the most tender kind of way.
This love illustrated a home, that was more than four walls.
This love exemplified beauty, that was always without words.
This love was not something that made me feel small. In fact, it was something that made me confident in seasons that tried to keep me small.

When I knew, I knew. And thats when I knew it was crucial to have, in a holy way. When I had the deep recognition that there was absolutely nobody better than this. When there was this keen understanding that there was absolutely nothing other than this that I would want to hold my attention. First, fall in the love with the One who made a way for us to love. And you'll have the answers to these questions before you can even ask.

Gosh. What an honor it is to know the one who made this what it is.

HONEST TRUTH

"Just think—you don't need a thing, you've got it all! All God's gifts are right in front of you as you wait expectantly for our Master Jesus to arrive on the scene for the Finale. And not only that, but God himself is right alongside to keep you steady and on track until things are all wrapped up by Jesus. God, who got you started in this spiritual adventure, shares with us the life of his Son and our Master Jesus. He will never give up on you. Never forget that."

1 Corinthians 1:9 (MSG)

CHALLENGE

You are not going to settle in your morals. Whatever those look like, live them out. You are not going to settle in your workplace. Wherever you are, go above and beyond what is expected of you. You are not going to settle in your thoughts. Start speaking to yourself what you want to see and watch what begins to shift. You are not going to settle in a relationship. The Lord is more than capable in this. Wait out for the person that triumphs any uncertainty. You are not going to settle with your dreams. If your dream is something you can accomplish on your own, dream something bigger. You are not going to settle in the core of who you are. Be bold. And note this — being bold does not always mean being loud. Whatever the day may hold, you hold onto what you know and you stand on what you want. One day you'll look back and say thank you to yourself. And you'll really mean it. No more settling, my friend.

Start small. Choose something that you know you have been settling in, and make the necessary steps in triumphing over it. You know what it is, just do yourself a favor and do it.

REFLECTION

I.   Are you currently entertaining something that you know God is not in? Why is stopping you from cutting it off?

II. Is there anything in your life that you have the "Eventually" mindset instead of what needs to be the "Immediately" mindset? What practical action steps are you going to take to move forward in the "Immediately"?

III. Have you ever settled for the average instead of waiting for God's best? Why do you think you chose the average? Knowing what you know now, how are you going to handle your future situations?

IV. How has your view of your personal family placed expectations on what your future family is or was suppose to look like?

V.   Describe your love for Jesus and who He is to you. Reflect on this.

CHAPTER 12
WHO I AM: THE ART OF CELEBRATION

Being in ministry, and being out of ministry. I learned the bottom line is that we do not owe a single person in this world anything except for love.

If we are not seeking to find the best in somebody than we are not living a life of love. If we are not putting our opinion of somebody to the side and choosing to see them for who they are then we cannot say we believe in grace. If we are not celebrating people's wins with them then we should not want to carry any of our own wins. If we are not meeting people where they are at then how can we expect them to know where they can be? If we are not small enough to stop what we are doing for somebody then we are not big enough to do anything for anybody.

Love is patient, love is kind. Love does not envy, love does not boast. Love is not proud. Love does not dishonor others. Love is not self-seeking. Love is not easily angered. Love keeps no record of wrongs. Love does not delight in evil but love rejoices with the truth. Love always protects, always trusts, always hopes, always perseveres.

We do not owe a single person in this world anything except for love.

CELEBRATE PEOPLE

One night in Atlanta, some friends and I were scooting around. We were scooting by all these homeless people and in something in me said to stop and talk to them. I do this a lot on my own time but not usually with friends. Don't get me wrong — I love the church. But there is something about the people who haven't made it to the church yet. When I see these people, they move my heart as if me and them are the only two people left in this world and as if it is my responsibility to stop and get to know their story. That night, we stopped. And we walked. And we met this man named Clark. This man has been homeless for years on end and when I tell you this man knew the word of God it blew my mind! He was teaching us things we didn't know. We were able to pray with him and as tears flooded down his face, it hit my soul that this is the Gospel. Not inside the walls, but here on these streets. I felt like a little girl in a candy shop running around the store and laughing with Clark as he picked out a few things we were able to get for him. I feel like we see the homeless and the lost and we sometimes forget that these people are humans with their own soul, too. They still have a purpose, too. They still are deserving someone to hear their story, too. These people are my why.

Once upon a time I hated humanity. Now, I firmly believe people are why I exist. People are my why. And I will celebrate us for the rest of my days. I will show up for people. I will love them as if it is the only thing I know how to do. And I believe that is how it ought to be. I believe in celebrating people, celebrating life, and celebrating our own mishaps. We live in a self orientated culture where typically the underlying motive is "me, me, me" when really, it should be "we". I want to use my life and my social media to bring celebration to the table and give it a permanent seat. Because we are all human and we all deserve to have someone cheering us on.

We aren't in a competition. Let's cheer each other on. Life is freaking hard sometimes. Let's use our failures and our indifferences for each other. If I win, you win. If you win, we win. Some of my absolute favorite memories are from conversations I started up with a stranger when I chose to celebrate the mess out of them. Some people look at you like you're crazy but almost every time there's been tears because of how uncommon it is for people to show love to people we do not know. Let's just get over ourselves honestly. If we are too big and full of ourselves to not notice somebody else and praise them, then we have nothing to offer to anybody. Let's choose to not be the reason why somebody feels alone.

CELEBRATE HONESTY

We are only as usable as we are honest. Honest with ourselves and honest with people. Being brave doesn't always mean being loud. And being meek doesn't always mean being quiet. There is a meeting place in the middle of these two and it is called honest. Honesty is not shouting high in our spotlight moments and it is not sitting silent in our messy seasons. Honesty is cherishing the ability to be present in both. Honesty does not walk into a room to conform to what is socially acceptable. Honesty sets up its own table and puts a welcome mat right in front of it. Honesty does not sit high and honesty does not sit low. Honesty sits down with an open heart. And in a totally opposite but holy turnaround, honesty influences others to love their honesty, too. Let's not be loud. Let's not be quiet. Let's just be honest.

Here I am, seven years later from when everything hit. Seven years ago I was kicked out of the church I now work at. Seven years ago depression suffocated my every breath. Seven years ago I was atheist. Seven years ago I had no hope. But here I am, showing up honest. I find myself teary-eyed almost everyday that this was the plan the Lord had all along. When nothing made sense, when everything hurt, when everything seemingly failed He was there. And now I'm here. I still don't have it altogether and I don't believe any of us will ever have it altogether. But all of us can show up honest. Because when we are honest God can work with that.

Honesty is vital in these moments of today. We live behind screens and sit before pulpits where it's been safe to shape perfection. But shaping perfection is not safe. Because of shaped perfection, humanity chases after something we will never achieve because of the very fact that we're human. We need raw, unlocked honesty. We need people who are proud to be human and who find it okay to show they don't always get it right. I don't know why we're so obsessed with perfection but what I do know is that I'm glad God is all about the messy. The ones who have real life weaknesses and the ones who trip when they walk by themselves. I can't find it in me to believe it's wrong that we doubt sometimes and that it's awful we say stupid things sometimes.

I think what really, truly, matters is if we have a heart for Him and if we're able to be honest with ourselves. And honest with people too. Because all these little mishaps - if your heart is towards Him, He's gonna help you through them. Life isn't about puffing up our "ooh and ahh" moments. I think life is about sharing our "How the heck do I get out of this" moments. And then gracefully sharing how God did in fact, faithfully bring us out of them. As He always does.

CELEBRATE GRACE

I don't know you. I don't know what your upbringing looked like. I don't know what your life looked/looks like at fifteen. I don't know how many times you've fallen flat on your face over the same struggle. I don't know how many times you have considered calling quits. I don't know how deeply you've ached. But I do know how I have. My upbringing was so ingenuine. At fifteen I was not sober and I was broken. I still fall flat on my face at times. I have ached, and I still ache sometimes. We're human. I know mine and you know yours.

But we both can know a God who calls us friend. I don't know where you're at or where you've been, but we both can know a God who's with us even when everything is blurry. We both can know a God who has orchestrated every detail for our life for something GOOD. We both can know a God who has seen us run away but who already knew where we would end up. We both can know a God who gives out chance after chance. We both can know a God is already on the floor ready to meet us before we even get there. We both can know a God who calms us in our frustration. We both can know a God who sees us. Who knows us. And who chooses us. Even when we can't see ourselves. Even when we don't know ourselves. Even when we would never choose ourselves. We both can know the God who picks us, every time. With no hesitation. Here's what I learned.

Good does not always shout good.
Good does not always fit comfortably.
Good is often hidden in really bad.
Good is not always an instant product that is tangible.
Good is not always aligned with my feelings.
Good is not a subcomponent of faultless.

In fact, I found the greatest good in the greatest mess.
In the middle of all the clutter, there was good.
In all of the restructuring, there was good.
In all of the opposite directions, there was good.
In all of the trips, there was good.

Good is not always loud and good is not always bright. On some days good is silent, and on some days good is cloudy. And here's the contradiction — those are the kind of days that i look back to, and see the greatest gifts in. How clever is God to hide good in all the places that shout bad.

Above it all, my soul has learned how to be more confident being uncertain. My spirit has learned how to be more comfortable being uncomfortable. And my heart has learned how to sing in the pit before it ever knew the palace. Now looking back; through the aches and through the promises proven true — I see radiance and I see glory. Because I see His hand in every mishap, every wound, every coincidence, and every triumph.

And behind it all, I see His goodness standing tall.

HONEST TRUTH

"Every time you cross my mind, I break out in exclamations of thanks to God. Each exclamation is a trigger to prayer. I find myself praying for you with a glad heart. I am so pleased that you have continued on in this with us, believing and proclaiming God's Message, from the day you heard it right up to the present. There has never been the slightest doubt in my mind that the God who started this great work in you would keep at it and bring it to a flourishing finish on the very day Christ Jesus appears."

Philippians 1:6 (MSG)

CHALLENGE

Be honest with yourself. Push the line of what's socially acceptable to be open about. Own your mishaps and use them to impact somebody else. Scan the room you walk into and pick somebody out to affirm and celebrate. Let's love the people who are overlooked. Let's cheer on the goals that seem unattainable. Let's give grace to humanity. Let's celebrate and love people so well that when they see us — they see Jesus.

REFLECTION

I.   What does celebration mean to you?

II.   What does celebrating people look like for you?

III. What does celebrating honesty mean to you?

IV.   What does celebrating grace mean to you?

V.   Why is celebration important?

VI.   How can we incorporate a culture of celebration wherever we go?

The Second Table

WE CHOOSE

We are not suppose to have it all together.

The only reason this truth is deep rooted within me is because at one time, I spent months - and I mean months, breaking myself in pieces trying to perfect every detail of my life. When I fell short, I panicked and grabbed whatever was in arms reach and I booked it. I'm not even a runner and I would sprint away. I hid for weeks mourning at what I had done. In disbelief I had fallen once again. Terrified to face the world again and was unsteady in the fact I had no idea what relationship with Jesus really meant.

You see, I sat down at this table once. Everyone was wearing masks and had their luggage next to them. However, it was zipped up so no one could see what was inside of this seemingly perfect looking baggage. They told me following Jesus meant to never do wrong. Because if you trip even a little, then that meant you never loved Him to begin with. And it wasn't long before I was shoved out from my seat. My life was too messy to try to put on a mask to fit in. My shortcomings were too heavy to try and carry them with me at the bottom of my bag. I wasn't comfortable in wearing a mask, because even if I tried, I knew what was really going on inside of me.

I walked alone for a bit, but I was not lonely. Just because you are alone at times, does not mean you are lonely. I was walking with Jesus trying to figure out what the heck it actually meant to be close to Him. Because I couldn't bring myself to believe perfection was it. While walking, I came across another table. Everyone was bare-faced and had their luggage next to them unzipped and wide opened. They were each taking turns reaching down into their baggage and pulling out their mistakes. And I watched each time as they tossed them behind their shoulder one by one.

This table. I sat down at this table, and I stayed. Without having to try to hide my shortcomings. Instead, we shared ours and even slapped our knees laughing about a few. Because some mistakes are so undoubtably insane that you have no choice but to laugh at them. This table didn't try to perfect themselves. They embraced our imperfectness. Then we moved forward to what was ahead. Not glued to our mess ups. You see, loving Jesus isn't contingent on whether or not you mess up. Loving Jesus is acknowledging you fell short, (even if it is yet again. Trust me, I know all about that) and choosing to get right back up. Christianity isn't perfection, my friend. You are not called to have it all together. You're going to mess up and you're going to fall.

Choose to get back up.

You can hide out and beat yourself up for messing up, of course. But when it's all said and done, God is still God. He forgives. He doesn't disown what is His. So yeah, you can mourn in it for weeks, but you will come to the conclusion that it's time to move forward because there is such ahead. But the question that sat deep in my soul in one season was, how much time are you going to let go to waste in the duration? He already forgave you. It's up to us when we choose to get back up. It's up to us to pull up our mistake, look at it, maybe laugh about it, and toss it over our shoulder. There's so much ahead. Now go get it, friend.

And hey, just for the books – I am still sitting at the second table. Everyday.

"Now it happened, as Jesus sat at the table in the house, that behold, many tax collectors and sinners came and sat down with Him and His disciples. And when the Pharisees saw it, they said to His disciples, "Why does your Teacher eat with tax collectors and sinners?" When Jesus heard that, He said to them, "Those who are well have no need of a physician, but those who are sick. But go and learn what this means: 'I desire mercy and not sacrifice.' For I did not come to call the righteous, but sinners, to repentance."

Matthew 9:9-13 (NKJV)

The Second Table

ABOUT THE AUTHOR

Hi. I'm Hope.

A lot of authors have this section written in third person but I couldn't bring myself to it. This is me, raw and authentic. I'm twenty two years old. I have been walking with Jesus for four years and I've been in ministry for six years. What an irony. Just because someone is in ministry doesn't always mean they're living right. I work at the church where I was kicked out of youth group seven years ago and it is one of my favorite things to share. I dropped out of High School in the tenth grade but now I am one of the directors for a college. I had a two in speech class my freshman year but now I speak and laugh about it. I have been writing for four years and I plan to continue to write.

I live in Gainesville, Georgia. The chicken capital of the United States and I always chuckle under my breath because this is so not my thing. My heart is for people. Specifically young adults, and specifically the people who haven't made it to church yet. There are a multitude of people to reach the people who are inside the walls of a church — my heart is for the people who haven't made it here yet. It is my goal to hear the story of every individual I meet because I believe everyone has a story worth hearing. It is my passion to celebrate the mistakes of life because we are who we are because of them. It is my heart to celebrate humanity because we all go through it and we all need a little celebration to keep moving.

I write and I speak, but my favorite thing to do is notice people. And love them in a way where all they can say is, "If this is how Jesus is… then I'm in."

Made in the USA
Monee, IL
21 July 2024

62391366R00121